HOW TO MAKE THE MOST OF YOUR TELESCOPE

Patrick Moore

Longman

LONGMAN GROUP LIMITED
Longman House, Burnt Mill, Harlow,
Essex CM20 2JE, England
and Associated Companies throughout the world.

First published 1985

ISBN 0 582 23535 9

Set in Matrix, SuperScan

Printed in Great Britain
at The Bath Press, Avon

British Library Cataloguing in Publication Data

Moore, Patrick
    How to make the most of your telescope.
    1. Astronomy — Observers' manuals
    I. Title
    522   QB64

    ISBN 0-582-23535-9

Star charts by Paul Doherty
and diagrams by Bob Chapman
Cover photograph by kind permission of
Daily Telegraph Colour Library.

Contents

Introduction:
The moving sky

Preface

When I was asked to write this book, I set out to provide something for the newcomer to astronomy who has managed to obtain a small, low-powered telescope. This is why I have deliberately not included any of the splendid pictures taken by using powerful instruments. I hope that everything shown and described here will be well within your reach, and that you will feel inclined to take matters further. After all, there can be no better hobby than astronomy.

In 1929, when I was at the early age of six, I began to take a lively interest in astronomy. It began simply because I picked up a book belonging to my mother, read it, and decided that it was worth following up. Now, well over half a century later, I have never regretted it. There is a great deal to be seen, and a great deal to do. In fact, astronomy is one of the few sciences in which the amateur can be really useful — always provided that he or she goes the right way about it.

I like to believe that I did so. My first step was to obtain a set of star charts, and start learning my way round the night sky. This does not take nearly so long as might be thought. Once the main star groups or constellations have been picked out, they can be used as pointers to all the rest. My next step was to read more books, until I had grasped the general idea of what astronomy is all about. I borrowed a pair of binoculars, and used them for some time, after which I started to think about buying a telescope.

The situation then was not the same as it is today. I saved up, and finally managed to buy a 75mm (three-inch) refracting telescope which I still have, and which I still use. It cost £7.50, although today the same telescope would cost in the region of £200.

What is the smallest astronomical telescope which is of real use? My opinion is that for a refractor, which collects its light with an object-glass, the minimum diameter of the object-glass should be 75mm (three inches); for a reflector, which uses a mirror, the mirror should be 150mm (six inches) across. Without spending a very large sum of money, then, you may have a choice between a much smaller telescope — say a 50mm or 65mm (two-inch or two-and-a-half-inch) refractor — or good binoculars. For reasons to be given later, I would vastly prefer the binoculars. But the fact remains that many people do own these very small telescopes, and they are better than nothing at all.

If you do decide upon a really satisfactory telescope, remember that your outlay of at least £200 is a "one-off". With care, the telescope will last for a lifetime, and there is no need to go on spending money as, for example, a photographer has to do. Also it is worth noting that a good telescope costs no more than a couple of first-class railway tickets between London and Scotland!

If you have bought a very small telescope, you will at least be able to use it to learn a good deal, and it will show you whether you are interested enough to make astronomy a life-long hobby. I wish you all success.

Basic facts

In this book I have not tried to write a full account of modern astronomy. I am concerned only with the newcomer who has obtained a very small telescope and is anxious to learn how to get the best out of it. But it is important to have a working knowledge of the main facts, so let us begin at the beginning.

The EARTH upon which we live is a planet, nearly 13 000km (8000 miles) in diameter, moving round the Sun at a distance of approximately 150 million km (93 million miles) in a period of one year (actually 365·25 days; it is that irritating quarter-day which forces us to have one Leap Year in four, giving February an extra day to keep the calendar properly in step). There are eight other planets: Mercury and Venus, which are closer to the Sun than we are, and Mars, Jupiter,

Saturn, Uranus, Neptune and Pluto, which are further away. Their revolution periods or "years" range from only 88 days for Mercury out to 248 years for the remote Pluto. Like the Earth, the planets have no light of their own. They shine by reflected sunlight, and look like stars.

The MOON is our companion in space, and stays together with us as we travel round the Sun. At its distance of only about 385 000 km (239 000 miles) – less than ten times the distance round the Earth's equator — it is much closer than any other natural body in the sky, and it looks more important than it really is. In fact, it is smaller than the Earth, with a diameter of only a little over 3200km (2000 miles), and it is much less massive; it "weighs" much less. If you could put the Earth into one pan of a gigantic pair of scales, you would need 81 Moons to balance it. It, too, depends upon reflecting the light of the Sun, and it has no atmosphere, so that its surface details can always be clearly seen.

The SUN is a star. It is rather surprising to find that it is not exceptional; it appears so magnificent in our skies only because it is so close to us on the scale of the universe. All the other stars are so much further away that it is awkward to measure their distances in kilometres or miles, just as it would be awkward to measure the distance between London and Bristol in centimetres or inches. Instead, astronomers use the "light-year". Light travels at 300 000km (186 000 miles) per second; in a year it covers rather less than ten million million km (six million million miles) and it is this unit which is known as the light year. The nearest star beyond the Sun is over four light years away, which works out at roughly 40 million million km (24 million million miles).

Scale models can be useful at times. If we represent the Earth—Sun distance by 2·5cm (one inch) — see *Fig 1* - the nearest star will be over 6·5km (four miles) away. Therefore, even though many stars are much larger and more luminous than the Sun, they appear as points of light. No telescope yet built will show a star as a definite disk.

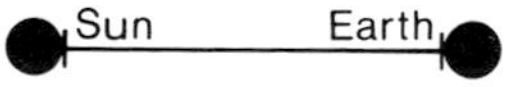

Because the stars are so far away, they do not seem to move noticeably with respect to each other. The constellations which we see today are practically the same as those which

Figure 1
If we represent the Earth-Sun distance as one inch, the nearest star will be over four miles away.

must have been seen by William the Conqueror or Julius Cæsar. On the other hand, the members of the Solar System — that is to say, the Sun's family of planets — are much nearer, and seem to wander slowly around from one constellation to another, though they always keep to certain definite zones.

The star-system of which our Sun is a member is known as the GALAXY. It contains about one hundred thousand million stars, and measures a hundred thousand light-years from one side to the other. It is a flattened system with a central bulge — I have often compared its shape with that of two fried eggs clapped together back to back. When we look along the main plane of the Galaxy, we see many stars in almost the same direction, and this is the cause of the lovely Milky Way band which stretches across the sky from one horizon to the other. Turn a telescope toward the Milky Way, and you will see so many stars that to count them would be impossible; but they are not genuinely crowded together, and direct collisions between two stars can hardly ever occur. There is no 3-D effect through a telescope, and appearances can be deceptive!

Seen from "above" or "below", the Galaxy would show up as a spiral system, like a Catherine-wheel. The Sun is not at the centre, but well out toward one edge. The distance between ourselves and the centre of the Galaxy is over 30 000 light-years. But even now we are only at the beginning of things. Beyond our Galaxy, so remote that in most cases their light takes many millions of years to reach us, we can see other galaxies, some of which (though by no means all) are spirals like our own. (See *Fig 40* on page 70 for a photograph of another galaxy.) They, too, contain thousands of millions of stars, and there is every reason to believe that many of these stars are the centres of planetary systems. There may well be many other Earths and many other intelligent beings, but unfortunately we have no proof, because no telescope yet built is powerful enough to show even a large planet moving round another star.

A word of warning here. Many books contain wonderful coloured pictures of the outer galaxies, and of objects such as gas-clouds or nebulæ. The colours are real enough, but they are too faint to be seen simply by looking through the eye-end of a telescope — just as it is impossible to tell a red car from a yellow one by moonlight; both will look grey. So it is very important not to be disappointed at what a small telescope will show you. Fortunately the members of the Solar System are more rewarding, and your telescope will give excellent views of the mountains and craters of the Moon, the dark spots on the Sun, and the rings of Saturn. **(The Sun, of course, must always be observed INDIRECTLY by using the telescope as a PROJECTOR (see page 22). To look straight at the Sun through any telescope, or even a pair of binoculars, will cause immediate and permanent blindness. I will have more to say about this later, but the danger is so great that I do not apologize for mentioning it at once.)**

Because the Earth spins on its axis from west to east in a period of 24 hours, the whole sky seems to rotate from east to west, carrying the Sun, Moon, stars and planets with it. The axis points northward to the north pole of the sky, which is close to a fairly bright star, Polaris or the Pole Star. Therefore, Polaris seems to remain almost motionless, with everything else revolving around it. Stars close to the pole simply move round and round without setting; for instance, the famous constellation of the Great Bear can always be seen whenever the sky is sufficiently dark and clear. Objects further away from the pole rise and set, so that they are not always on view. Also, the sky does not look the same from all places on Earth. Go to Australia, for instance, and you will never see Polaris, because it stays below the horizon all the time.

Recording observations

I am often asked about the best way of recording one's observations. If a telescope is being used to make an observation or a drawing, always include: your name, the name of the object you are observing, the time in Greenwich Mean Time — GMT (never use Summer Time), the condition of the sky, the seeing (on a scale from 1 to 5, 1 being "perfect" and 5 "very poor"), the telescope used, the magnification of eyepiece used, and any other notes which seem to be appropriate.

It is probably best to keep a separate notebook for each object: one for the Moon, one for Jupiter, one for variable stars and so on, as well as a book for general comments. Never throw an observation away, because you never know when it may suddenly become important.

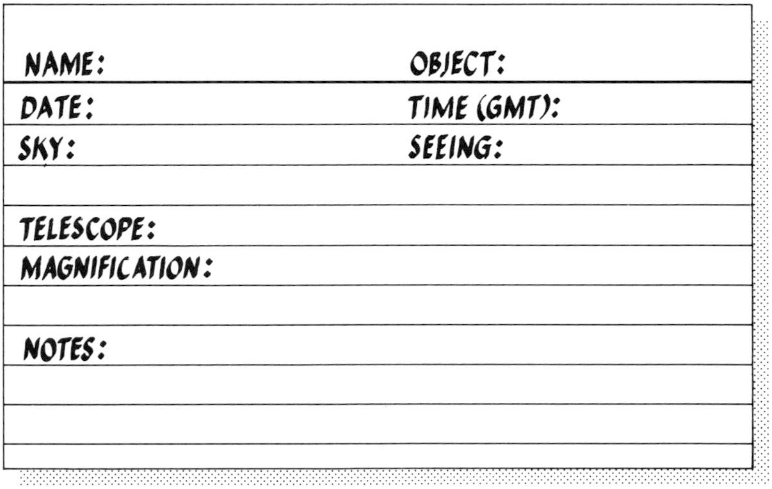

NAME:	OBJECT:
DATE:	TIME (GMT):
SKY:	SEEING:
TELESCOPE:	
MAGNIFICATION:	
NOTES:	

Figure 2
Never throw an observation away.

Photography

Photographs taken with a small, undriven telescope are never of much use, and it is really rather pointless to try unless you have at least a three-inch refractor or six-inch reflector, firmly and equatorially mounted, and clock-driven (see *Fig 8* on page 18).

Your telescope and what it can do

Astronomy is open to everybody. There is plenty to be seen with the naked eye, and — as I have said — the first step should be to learn the constellation patterns, but eventually comes the question of using a telescope.

Magnification

TELESCOPES are of two kinds: REFRACTORS and REFLECTORS. The refractor collects its light by using a lens known as an object-glass or objective, while the reflector uses a specially-shaped mirror. The size of the telescope is given according to the diameter of the main light-collector — called the aperture. I have always said that the smallest telescope which is of real use in astronomy is either a 75mm (three-inch) refractor (that is to say, a refractor with an object-glass 75mm (three inches) in diameter) or else a 150mm (six-inch) reflector (a telescope with a mirror 150mm (six inches) in diameter). However, many smaller telescopes are on the market, mainly refractors with apertures of 50 to 65mm (two to two and a half inches), and many newcomers to astronomy own them.

Before going on, something more must be said about BINOCULARS, which are much more useful astronomically than is often believed. The sad fact is that good astronomical tele-scopes are not cheap. The days when one could find a useful second-hand telescope for a few pounds have long since passed and the newcomer who wants to be really well equipped will have to spend at least £200, while £300 is a more realistic sum. There are many people who do not want to spend over £200, or else simply cannot afford it. This is where personal opinions are all-important, and all I can do is to give my own views, although other people may well dis-agree. With only a limited sum of money to spend (say

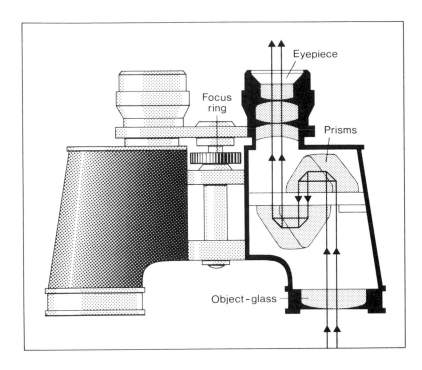

Figure 3
Binoculars

between £10 and £60) I would prefer good binoculars to a very small telescope, because binoculars are easy to handle, and have most of the advantages of a small telescope apart from sheer magnification. And, of course, they can be used for ordinary daytime viewing as well (ships out to sea, birds, and so on) whereas the small astronomical telescope cannot, chiefly because it is bound to have a very small field of view.

A pair of binoculars is really made up of two small refractors paired up together, so that both of one's eyes can be used (see *Fig 3*). The diameters of the two object-glasses are given in millimetres. Thus a pair of 7×50 binoculars indicates that the magnification is seven times, and that each object-glass is 50mm across. Binoculars of this type give wide fields, and will show much of interest in the night sky — the craters of the Moon, for example, and many glorious star-fields. With binoculars giving a magnification of over 12, the field of view becomes inconveniently small, and the instrument becomes so heavy that it is usually helpful to make a mounting of some sort; but any magnification betwen 7 and 12 is acceptable. I admit to being a binocular enthusiast. However, for the moment let us turn back to small telescopes, and see what we can expect.

Refractors

In a refractor, the light from the object being observed passes through the object-glass. The light-rays are bunched up and are brought together at the focus, where an image of the object is formed. This image is then enlarged by a second, smaller lens called an eyepiece, which is really nothing more nor less than a special type of magnifying-glass. Note that the enlargement is done by the eyepiece: light-collection depends upon the object-glass. Of course, the larger the object-glass, the more light is available so that higher magnifications can be used. Eyepieces can be changed, and it is wise to have several, giving different powers.

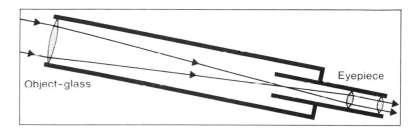

Figure 4
The refractor

It is a general rule that one can use a magnification of fifty for each 25mm (one inch) in the diameter of the light-collector (or aperture). Thus a 50mm (two-inch) refractor should bear a maximum power of $2 \times 50 = 100$ times, while a 75mm (three-inch) will bear $3 \times 50 = 150$ times. (It must be admitted that many advertisements are misleading: anyone who hopes to use a magnification of over 200 on a 65mm (two-and-a-half-inch) refractor, for instance, is doomed to disappointment, because the image produced will be hopelessly faint.)

Remember that with a small astromonical telescope, the field of view will be very narrow. Also, the image produced will be upside-down. It is possible to add an extra lens to turn the image upright again (as is always done with binoculars), but every time a ray of light is passed through a lens it is slightly weakened, and for astromonical purposes this is a bad thing, so that the correcting lenses are usually left out. After all, it does not in the least matter whether you see the Moon upside-down or erect.

Reflectors

So far I have been talking about small refractors, because these are the telescopes generally used by newcomers to astronomy. The principle of the reflector is different. In the common form (known as the Newtonian, because the system was first worked out by Isaac Newton over 300 years ago), the light falls upon the curved mirror and is reflected back up the open tube onto a second, small flat mirror, placed at an angle to it of 45°. The flat mirror directs the rays into the side wall of the tube, where they are brought to focus and the image is magnified by an eyepiece fitted into the side.

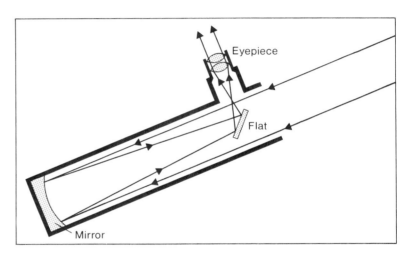

Figure 5
The Newtonian
reflector

Size for size, a reflector is not so powerful as a refractor; for instance, a 75mm (three-inch) Newtonian reflector is too small to be useful. The smallest reflectors generally sold have mirrors 115mm (four and a half inches) in diameter. Since it is awkward to aim a telescope when one has to look into the side instead of straight up the tube, a finder or a gun-sight arrangement is very useful, though not essential.

Reflectors are cheaper than refractors, and they do have their advantages, particularly with larger instruments. A 150mm (six-inch) reflector is not likely to cost more than £300, but a 150mm (six-inch) refractor would run to well over £1000. Also, no refractor of aperture over 100mm (four inches) is really portable, whereas a 115mm (four-and-a-half-inch) or even a 150mm (six-inch) reflector can fit into the boot of a car, together with its mounting.

14

Generally, the remarks I have made about refractors apply also to reflectors, but there are extra problems, because the reflector is much more likely to go out of adjustment. Unless the mirrors are correctly lined up, it will be impossible to bring the target object to focus. To align the mirrors (or collimate them, to use the technical term), first make sure that the main mirror is firmly in position; then look through the eyepiece holder, without using an actual eyepiece, and adjust the flat mirror until the image is central. If this cannot be done, you will have to shift the main mirror slightly. Again, trial and error is the only method.

The mirror of a small reflector will be made of glass, coated with a thin layer of silver or (more usually) aluminium to make it reflective. After a while it will be found that the mirror is starting to look dull or even stained in places. A slight dimming or stain is not usually worth bothering about, but eventually the mirror will have to be given a fresh coating of aluminium. This is not easily done at home because it needs special equipment, and so the main mirror — perhaps the flat one also — should be taken to an optical firm. Luckily re-coating does not cost much, and under normal conditions it need be done only once every two or three years.

If the mirror becomes dusty, never rub it; if you do, you will remove the delicate aluminium coating, which is only a fraction of a millimetre thick. Never rub moisture away; simply bring the mirror indoors and let the moisture evaporate. A hair-dryer can be effective for this.

Even when the mirrors are firmly mounted, they are still liable to go out of adjustment, and periodically re-collimation is needed. All in all, a reflector needs much more care and maintenance than a refractor.

Many reflectors have open-work skeleton tubes, which makes them lighter and more portable. If the tube is solid, it is a good idea to have a flap or "window" at the lower end, so that a cap can be placed over the main mirror when the telescope is not in use. If no cap has been provided, make one out of cardboard (or a suitably-sized cake-tin lid) and cover the inside with blotting paper. Do not force the cap down on to the mirror; leave it so that it barely touches. Some people even prefer to leave a millimetre or two between the mirror surface and the blotting paper inside the cover.

One major advantage of a reflector is that the eyepiece is near the top end of the tube, and with an altazimuth mounting (see below) it is always at a convenient angle. With a refractor, the eyepiece is at the bottom end, and when the target object is high in the sky the eyepiece will be so low down that the observer will have to bend awkwardly to reach it. (The best remedy here is to make some sort of rigid platform, so that the tripod can be set on it to make the eyepiece easier to reach.) (See also page 75)

Mounting

The other really important point is that the telescope must be firmly mounted. Spidery, quivering tripods are of no use at all. As soon as you get your target into the field of view it will dance about as soon as the telescope is shaken by the slightest breeze. The mounting must be really rigid. The tripod of my three-inch refractor, shown in *Fig 6*, is quite satisfactory, and is also fairly easy to carry around, but anything less substantial is bound to cause trouble. Some small refractors are even sold on mountings of the pillar-and-claw type, designed to be put down on a table or a bench (see *Fig 7*). I can only say that the average pillar-and-claw stand is about as rigid as a blancmange, and should be avoided. Fortunately, it is an easy matter to replace the pillar-and-claw with a proper tripod.

A simple tripod mounting is called an altazimuth, because the telescope can be moved freely both in *alt*itude and in *azimuth* (direction). There are more complicated mountings for larger telescopes, but I do not propose to say much about them here, because they are not usually found with refractors below 75mm (three inches) aperture. The same applies to what are called slow motion controls. Because the sky moves round from east to west, the target object is shifting all the time. The telescope can be guided by hand so as to keep the target in view, but it is not easy to avoid jerking, and some kind of mechanical device is very convenient.

Figure 6
The telescope must
be firmly mounted.

Figure 7
The average pillar-
and-claw stand is
about as rigid as a
blancmange.

Figure 8
The Henry Brinton
Telescope at Selsey.
Note the slow motion
controls and "finder"
telescope.

Of course there are all sorts of "extras". A very small telescope
can be mounted on the tube of the main instrument to act as a
finder; if it has a very low magnification and a very wide field,
it is easy to bring the target object into the centre of the finder-
field, so that if everything is properly lined up the object will
then also be in the field of the main telescope. Even a simple
arrangement of two pins stuck on the tube and aligned like a
gun-sight, without a lens at all, will give you the direction.

Focusing

When the telescope is ready for use, and has been aimed at
the target object, the first need is to focus up. By this, I mean
altering the position of the eyepiece until the object appears
sharp and clear-cut. The eyepiece can be pushed in or pulled
out, and focusing is a matter of trial and error; also, no two
people have exactly the same focus. (People who use specta-
cles will generally do better to take them off.) A star is so far
away that it appears as a dot of light; the smaller it looks, the

better you are seeing it. If the telescope shows a star as a blurred, shimmering ball, then the focus is wrong, and must be adjusted. The Moon shows a tremendous amount of detail, and the best advice here is to focus up on a lunar crater which is partly filled with shadow. With the planets, adjust the focus until the disk has sharp edges — though I admit that this is not always possible; you need very calm, steady air to observe the planets well.

Unfortunately, I have found that some small refractors, bought new, are provided with higher-power eyepieces which obstinately refuse to focus. Generally, this is because they cannot be pulled out far enough, and the remedy is to construct an extension tube out of thick cardboard so that the eyepiece can be held at a sufficient distance from the end of the main tube. This is a problem which never ought to occur, but sometimes does.

Care and maintenance

The main advantage of a small refractor is that once it has been mounted and adjusted, there is very little to go wrong. Always keep the object-glass covered with a cap when the telescope is not in use, to keep off both dust and damp; a cap is easy to make — a coffee-tin lid is often ideal, and lining it with blotting paper will help. If the object-glass does become dirty, never rub it hard. Wiping very gently with a soft silk rag is acceptable, though a better method in most cases is to borrow a hair-dryer and blow a current of air across the lens. Moisture is not really a problem, because when the telescope is brought back indoors the moisture will evaporate. However, it sometimes happens that when observations are being made in damp air, the object-glass becomes covered with dew. To stop this, simply make a cardboard extension tube and fasten it over the end of the telescope tube itself.

Provided that reasonable care is taken, a refractor needs no maintenance apart from making sure that the mechanical parts do not become rusty or stiff. If the telescope is dropped, and the object-glass is jolted out of position, it is wise to take the telescope to an optical expert rather than try to wrench the lens back into place.

Where to take your telescope

Observing from indoors is not a good idea. The inside of a house is likely to be warmer than the air outside, and if a telescope is poked through an open window it will be looking through a layer of swirling, disturbed air as the warm and cold regions meet, so that it will be hopeless trying to focus properly. Since a small refractor is portable, take it out of doors, preferably in a garden, if you have one, and as far away from the house as you can. Trees are always a nuisance — and it is always found that any tall tree lies in the most inconvenient position possible. Even worse is the trouble caused by artificial lights. People who live in city centres are at a hopeless disadvantage, and it is often impossible to see the stars even when the sky is cloudless. There is absolutely no remedy for this except to select the darkest position obtainable, and make the best of a bad job. Luckily a small refractor telescope can be carried in a car, and taken to a site well away from the glare.

For the do-it-yourself enthusiast

Finally, what about making your own telescope if you cannot afford to buy one? Years ago it was possible to buy cheap lenses from opticians and mount them in cardboard tubes, while a 50mm (two-inch) lens served for the eyepiece and a jeweller's eyepiece could be used as a magnifier. Unfortunately these lenses are now much less easy to find and there is no point in buying a proper astronomical object-glass on its own. On the other hand, there are many amateurs who construct their own reflectors, even grinding the mirrors. This is definitely quite a task and not something to be attempted when school examinations loom ahead! Probably the best way to obtain a useful telescope at reasonably low cost is to buy the optics for a reflector and then make your own mounting*. This cuts the cost down to a few tens of pounds. But this is not the place to go into the details of DIY, so let us assume that we have equipped ourselves with a small telescope, and see the uses to which it can be put.

*If you are interested in doing this, you will find the book *Make Your Own Telescope* by Reg Spry (Sidgwick & Jackson) useful reading.

Programme 1:
Observing the Sun

The one object which can be well seen even from a city centre is the Sun, but I must again give the **SERIOUS WARNING made in the Introduction: NEVER LOOK AT THE SUN DIRECTLY THROUGH ANY TELESCOPE OR BINOCULARS.** It is even unwise to stare straight at the Sun with the naked eye. The reason is obvious enough. The Sun is not only very brilliant, but also very hot, and one need only look back at the old Boy Scout method of starting a camp fire by using a magnifying-glass to focus the Sun's rays on to a piece of dry vegetation. The heat will make the material burst into flames. If you look at the Sun through a telescope, the heat will be focused on to your eye, and the result will be permanent blindness. This is not over-caution: I know of two people who have actually been blinded in this way.

Most unfortunately, some small telescopes are sold together with what are called "sun filters": these are dark glasses which — it is claimed   can be screwed over the telescope eyepiece to cut down the sunlight and make direct viewing safe. **THIS IS QUITE DEFINITELY NOT TRUE,** and these "sun filters" **SHOULD NEVER BE USED.** They cannot give full protection, and in any case they are always liable to splinter suddenly, so that you will not have enough time to move your eye out of the danger zone. If your telescope does have such a sun filter, throw it away!

Characteristics of the Sun

The Sun may be nothing more than an ordinary star, but it has a surface temperature of almost six million degrees Centigrade, and near its core the temperature rises to the almost unbelievable value of at least 14 million degrees. The Sun is made of gas. It is not "burning" in the usual sense of the word, but is shining by a quite different process. Deep inside it there is a great deal of the lightest of all the elements, hydrogen (one of the elements making up water; the chemical formula H_2O means that a molecule or atom-group of water is made up of two "bits" or atoms of hydrogen together with one atom of oxygen). Near the Sun's centre, hydrogen is being changed into another element, helium. It takes four "bits" of hydrogen to make one "bit" of helium; every time this happens, a little energy is set free and a little mass is lost. It is this energy which keeps the Sun shining. The loss of mass (or "weight", if you like) amounts to four million tons every second, so that the Sun "weighs" much less now than it did when you started reading this page. Fortunately there is no reason to be alarmed. The Sun is so massive that it will not change much for at least five thousand million years in the future.

Projecting the Sun's image

There is only one golden rule for looking directly at the Sun through a telescope or binoculars: **DON'T,** even when the Sun is low over a misty horizon and looks very pale and weak.

This does not mean that the Sun cannot be studied telescopically. Of course it can, but the observer's eye should never be anywhere near the eyepiece of the telescope.

The only safe method is to use the telescope as a projector. (Binoculars are not suitable for this.) First, point the telescope toward the Sun with the cardboard or tin cap kept well over the object-glass or mirror: this can be done easily enough by taking a squint along the tube of either the main telescope or the finder (not through the finder itself). Then remove the cap, and hold or fix a piece of white paper or card behind the eyepiece, moving it around until the image of the Sun is shown sharply and clearly. Once the telescope has been uncapped, never put your eye anywhere near the eyepiece.

Sunspots

The bright surface of the Sun, known to astronomers as the photosphere, is not always blank. Very often it shows dark

Figure 9
Projecting the sun with my three-inch refractor

patches known as sunspots, which are not really black, but appear so because they are about 2000 degrees cooler than the surrounding surface. Spots often appear in groups. A large spot has a dark central portion or umbra, surrounded by a lighter area known as penumbra. Sometimes the spots are circular, sometimes they are very irregular in shape. They will show up well on your white screen, and it is always interesting to draw them. (It is generally a good idea to fix a shield or shade round the upper part of the telescope so that it casts its shadow on to your screen; this makes the spots show up much more clearly.)

No spot lasts for more than a few weeks or months, and the shapes and sizes of any group change from one day to

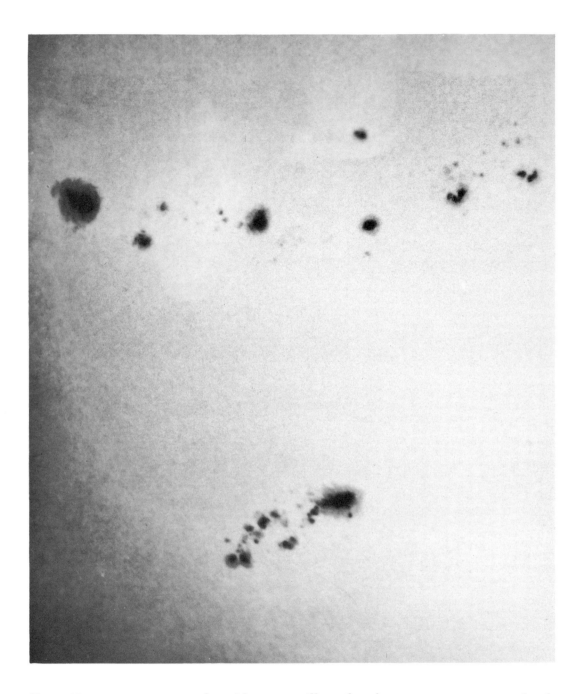

Figure 10
The bright surface of the Sun shows dark patches known as sunspots.

another. Also, you will see that the spots seem to move slowly across the Sun's face from one side to the other — not over a few minutes, of course, but again from one day to the next. This is because the Sun is spinning round. The Earth rotates once in 24 hours; the Sun takes about a month, so that a spot needs about two weeks to cross one side of the disk to the

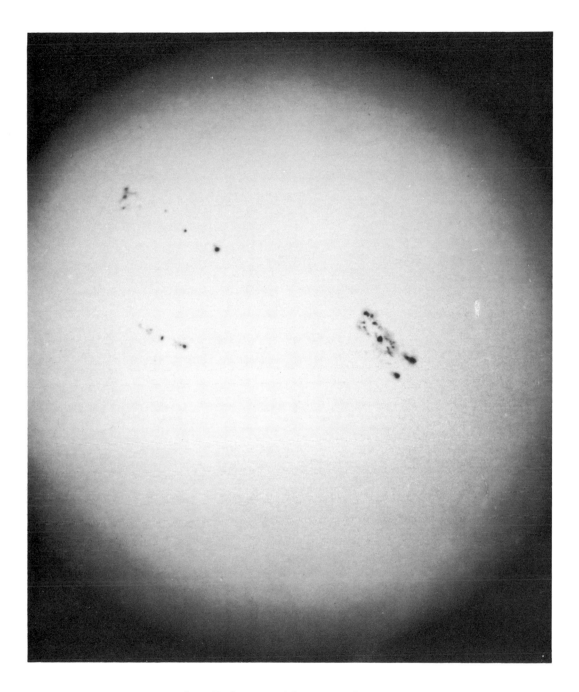

Figure 11
Spots often appear in
groups.

other. It then vanishes over the sun's edge or limb; if it lasts for long enough, it will reappear at the opposite limb about a fortnight later. (I say "about" because the Sun does not spin in a way that a solid body such as the Earth will do. The Sun's equator spins more quickly than the regions closer to its poles.)

25

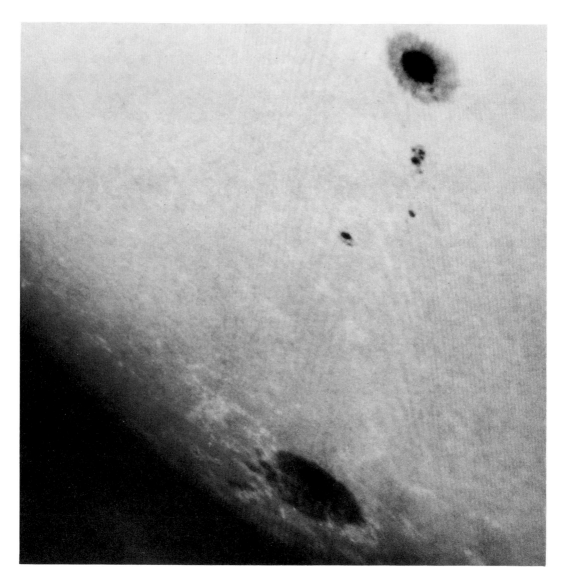

Figure 12
When a spot is near the Sun's edge it will be foreshortened.

When a spot or spot-group is near the Sun's edge, it will be foreshortened, so that a circular spot will appear as an oval. It is also possible to see very bright areas, usually around spot-groups; these are known as faculae, from the Latin word meaning "torches", and these are bright gases lying above the main surface.

The Sun is not always active. Every 11 years or so there is a solar maximum, when many spot-groups may be seen at the same time. Activity then dies slowly down until at solar mini-mum there may be days or even weeks when no spots are seen at all, after which activity starts to build up again. The average length between one maximum and the next is 11 years, but the solar cycle is not perfectly regular. The last maximum was that of 1980, and the next is expected about 1991, so that during the mid-1980s there will be comparatively few spots.

Aurora Borealis (Northern Lights)

Figure 13
The Northern Lights may be brilliantly coloured and change quickly over a few minutes.

Active sun spots send out streams of electrically-charged particles which cross the 150 million km (93 million mile) gap between the Sun and the Earth and dash into the upper air, making it glow and causing the lovely displays of Northern Lights or Polar Lights. These auroræ are not commonly viewed from latitudes below 60° north because the particles, being electrified, make for the Earth's magnetic poles. It is not often that there are good displays from southern England, but in Scotland (which is much closer to the magnetic pole) auroræ are quite frequent, particularly around the time of the solar maximum activity, mentioned in the previous

section. People living in (or visiting) the Orkneys or the Shetlands will get even better displays, but you have to be in places like Norway, Greenland or Alaska to see them at their most spectacular. As no telescope is needed to watch auroræ, which may be brilliantly coloured and change quickly over a period of a few minutes, they are included here mainly as a bonus for some of you who will find yourselves watching the night sky at the right time in the right place.

Eclipses of the Sun

Because the Earth moves round the Sun and the Moon moves round the Earth, it must sometimes happen that the Moon will move directly in front of the Sun, blotting out the sunlight and causing what is known as a solar eclipse. The Moon has no light of its own, and at the time of an eclipse its night side is turned toward us, so that the Moon itself cannot be seen at all.

Remember, at all times, that even when the Sun is partly hidden it is still dangerous. During the last partial eclipse to be visible from Britain there were many cases of people who damaged their eyes permanently by staring straight at it. With the naked eye, it is only safe to look at an eclipse for a few seconds by holding up a piece of very dark glass in front of your eye, but even then be very careful indeed — and, as always, never look directly through a telescope or binoculars. A partly-eclipsed Sun can blind you just as quickly as a Sun which is fully visible. To observe an eclipse, use the projection method in the ordinary way.

At a total eclipse the sight is magnificent. The Moon looks just big enough to cover the Sun completely, and as soon as the lining up is exact the Sun's outer atmosphere, known as the corona, flashes into view, while the sky becomes so dark that stars can be seen.

Unfortunately total eclipses are rare as seen from any particular point on the Earth. The last to be seen in England was that of 1927, and the next will not be until 11th August 1999, when a total eclipse will be visible from Cornwall. Other parts of the world are luckier. For instance, a total eclipse was seen

Figure 14
At a total eclipse the Sun's outer atmosphere, known as the corona, flashes into view.

in the Pacific area on 11th June 1983, and one was visible from Australia on 22nd November 1984.

Eclipses of the Sun

1985	May 19	Partial	Invisible in Britain
	November 12	Total	Invisible in Britain
1986	April 9	Partial	Invisible in Britain
	October 3	Total/annular	Invisible in Britain
1987	March 29	Total/annular	Invisible in Britain
	September 23	Annular	Invisible in Britain
1988	March 18	Total	Invisible in Britain

Figure 15

At a partial eclipse, when only a portion of the Sun is covered up, the appearance is that of a "bit" out of the Sun, and since no eclipse lasts for more than a few hours it is very interesting to make regular drawings to show when any spots on the Sun's face are covered and then uncovered again. Although partial eclipses are more common, they are much less dramatic than total eclipses because the corona cannot be seen.

Programme 2:
Observing the Moon

The Moon is certainly the most interesting of all objects for the owner of a very small telescope. Here there is no danger to the eye. The Moon looks brilliant, and it may dazzle you, but it sends us practically no heat, and direct observation is quite safe.

Since the Moon shines only by reflected sunlight, only part of it can be lit up at any one time — that part which is turned toward the Sun — and this is why the Moon shows us its regular phases, or changes of shape, from new to full. When it is almost between the Sun and the Earth (position 1 in *Fig 16*) its dark side faces in our direction; the Moon is then "new" and cannot be seen — unless the lining-up between Sun and Earth is exact, which would give us a solar eclipse.

Phases of the Moon

As the Moon moves along in its orbit, more of the sunlit side begins to show.

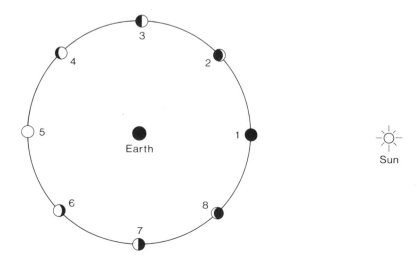

Figure 16
Phases of the Moon

At position 2: the Moon becomes a crescent.

At position 3: half Moon

At position 4: "gibbous", between half and full

At position 5: the Moon is full, the whole of the sunlit side
facing us.

After which, things happen in the reverse order.

Position 6: "gibbous"

Position 7: half Moon

Position 8: crescent

The Moon returns to new (position 1).

The interval between one new moon and the next is just over 29 days, so that generally there is one new Moon and one full Moon each month.

The Moon takes exactly the same time to spin once on its axis. The best way to show what is meant is to walk round a chair, turning as you go and keeping your eyes toward the chair. If you do this, you will make one complete turn 'on your axis' because during your walk you will face every wall of the room; but anyone sitting on the chair will never see the back of your neck.

The "back" of the Moon

From the Earth, we never see the "back" of the Moon, and until 1959, when the Russians sent an unmanned spaceship on a round trip to take photographs, we had no real idea of what the hidden areas were like. They proved to be just as rough and crater-scarred as the parts of the Moon which we have always been able to see, though there were no really large grey plains.

Eclipses of the Moon

At full Moon it sometimes happens that the Moon passes into the cone of shadow cast by the Earth and its sunlight is temporarily cut off. The result is a lunar eclipse, which may be either total or partial. The Moon becomes dim, often coppery-coloured, before it passes out of the shadow again. The

spectacle is beautiful although not astronomically important. The Moon does not generally disappear completely,
because some of the Sun's rays are bent on to it by way of the
layer of atmosphere surrounding the Earth. Lunar eclipses
are more frequent than those of the Sun, because when a
lunar eclipse occurs it can be seen from any place on Earth
where the Moon is above the horizon.

Eclipses of the Moon

1985	May 4	Total
	October 28	Total
1986	April 24	Total
	October 17	Total
1987	October 7	Partial (one per cent eclipsed)
1988	August 27	Partial (30 per cent eclipsed)

Figure 17
Being revised

First look at the Moon's surface

Even with the naked eye, dark patches can be seen on the
Moon's surface, and because the Moon has no atmosphere
the scene is always sharp and clear. The patches were once
thought to be seas, and were given romantic names which we
still use: the Sea of Clouds, the Ocean of Storms, the Bay of
Rainbows and so on. But without air, there can be no water,
and the Moon's "seas" are great dry plains with no moisture
in them. There has never been any water on the Moon.

As soon as a telescope is used, the Moon's surface is seen to
be crowded with detail. There are mountains, hills and valleys, and there are thousands of craters — walled circular formations with sunken floors and often with central mountains or groups of mountains. The craters are everywhere;
they cluster thickly on the bright highlands of the Moon, and
are also to be found on the waterless seas. They break into
each other and form complicated groups; there are pairs of
craters, and also lines of huge walled formations. The largest
craters are well over 160km (100 miles) in diameter.

Oddly enough, full moon is the very worst time to start
observing. This is because the sunlight is coming "straight
down" on to the Moon's surface, and the mountains and the

crater walls cast almost no shadows. Everything seems to be a jumble, and there are systems of bright streaks or rays which stretch across the surface for hundreds of kilometres, covering up the craters and making them hard to recognize. It is much better to start when the Moon is a crescent or half. Look first along the "terminator", or boundary between the sunlit and night hemispheres, where the Sun is just rising or setting over that area of the Moon (rising between new and full, or setting between full and new). The craters look splendid, with dark shadows thrown across their floors. Sometimes, too, a mountain-top will catch the sunlight before the lower-lying ground below, and will appear as a starlike point well clear of the rest of the Moon.

The craters have been named in honour of famous men and women of the past, usually astronomers, and are shown by name on the published Moon maps. Once recognized, they can be identified again, but it is true that their general appearance alters quickly with the changing angle of sunlight. A crater which appears very conspicuous when on the terminator may be hard to find a few nights later, when the Sun has risen higher over it and the shadows are much shorter.

There is one useful fact which makes identifying the craters easier than it would otherwise be: they always remain in the same positions on the Moon's face (or practically so) relative to the observer. This is because the Moon always keeps the same hemisphere turned towards us. Thus the crater Plato is always near the northern edge (that is to say, using an ordinary astronomical telescope which turns the image on its head, in the lower part of the Moon) while the ray-crater Tycho is not far from the southern edge (the upper part, viewed through the telescope).

Tasks: Aristarchus, Plato, Tycho, Copernicus

The method which I followed when I started to observe the Moon was to take an outline map of the Moon, and then set out to draw the craters which were best shown. I then made further drawings of the same craters over the next few nights, so that I could follow the changes in shadow and see how the craters seemed to change in appearance. Before long I was able to find my way around the Moon's surface, and things were made easier because there are some craters which can always be identified at once — because they are either exceptionally bright or else exceptionally dark.

ARISTARCHUS can be found in the grey plain of the Ocean of Storms. It has brilliant walls and central mountain and although only 37km (23 miles) in diameter it can never be overlooked when it is lit up by the Sun. It can even be seen on the night side of the Moon, by light reflected on to the Moon from the Earth — an effect nearly always visible when the Moon is a slender crescent.

PLATO, 100km (60 miles) in diameter, lies on the edge of the Sea of Showers. It has a more or less level floor, so dark grey in colour that it is always easy to locate.

TYCHO and COPERNICUS have two main ray systems which radiate from them, the first in the southern uplands, the second nearer the Moon's equator. There are many minor ray centres as well. Tycho is 87km (54 miles) in diameter.

Visiting the Moon

As everyone knows, men have been to the Moon. Twelve astronauts have walked among the lunar rocks: the first was Neil Armstrong in 1969, the most recent and perhaps the last, Eugene Cernan in 1972. They found a world which was full of interest. The sky was black even with the Sun high in the sky; the Earth was magnificent, and the pull of gravity was so weak that a human body had only one-sixth of its usual weight. There was no air, water or life; when the astronauts set up flags, there was no wind to make them flutter. The Moon is a world where almost nothing happens, and where nothing has happened for at least 1000 million years in the past. The rocks brought back proved to be volcanic, which was no surprise, and some of them were very old — as old, indeed, as the most ancient rocks of Earth. No doubt people will go back to the Moon in the future, and quite possibly set up a proper Lunar Base. Meanwhile, there is always much to see with your telescope, and it does not take long to become really familiar with the surface of the Moon.

Programme 3:
Observing the Planets

The planets of the Sun's family are fascinating worlds. Of course they are not nearly so easy to study as the Moon, because they are so much further away: even Venus, the closest of them, is always at least a hundred times as remote as the Moon. Also, they revolve round the Sun, not round the Earth, so that they are not always visible. Sometimes they may be almost out of view for months at a time. But each has its own special points of interest, and the brighter ones at least are rewarding objects in a small telescope.

The Solar System

The Solar System is divided into two parts. First we have four fairly small, solid planets: Mercury, Venus, the Earth and Mars. Beyond Mars there is a wide gap, in which move thousands of dwarf worlds known as the minor planets or asteroids. Further out we come to the giants, Jupiter, Saturn, Uranus and Neptune, all of which are much larger than the Earth, and have surfaces which are made up of gas rather than solid rock. The planetary family is completed by Pluto, which is a strange little body apparently in a class of its own. It was discovered as recently as 1930, and is too faint to be seen at all except with a large telescope, so that for the moment it does not concern us.

Of the other planets, Mercury is not particularly easy to find, because it always keeps so close to the Sun. Venus is brilliant — indeed, much brighter than anything else in the sky apart from the Sun and the Moon. At its best I have seen it actually cast shadows. Mars, Jupiter and Saturn are all bright, but Uranus is at the limit of naked-eye visibility, and to see Neptune at all, you need binoculars or a telescope.

To be honest, I would say that of these planets only Jupiter and Saturn are really well seen with small telescopes, though Mars and Venus are worth looking at. So let us examine the planets one by one, and decide the best way to observe them with our limited equipment.

Mercury and Venus

Being closer to the Sun than we are, they have their own way of behaving. They always stay in the same part of the sky as the Sun, and are at their best only when in the western sky after sunset or in the eastern sky before dawn. Also, they show phases in the same way as those of the Moon, and for much the same reason. When either Mercury or Venus is almost between the Earth and the Sun (position 1 in *Fig 18*) its dark or night side faces us, and we cannot see it at all. By the time either of them has reached position 2 it appears as a half. At position 3 it is full, with its daylit side facing us, but this is not of much help, because the planet is almost behind the Sun and is completely drowned by the brightness of the sky. It then become gibbous, shrinking to a half (position 4) before returning to new.

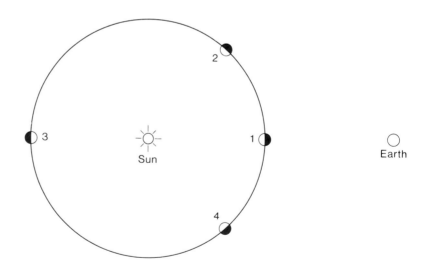

Figure 18
Phases of Mercury and Venus.

The trouble about Mercury is that it is a small world, not a great deal larger than the Moon; its diameter is 4875 km (3030 miles). When found, it looks quite bright, but again I must give a warning. **Never use binoculars or a telescope to search for Mercury unless the Sun is completely below the**

horizon, because there is always the risk of looking straight at the Sun by mistake.

When Mercury has been found, your telescope will show its phase, but nothing more. There is always satisfaction to be gained in locating Mercury; on average it can be seen with the naked eye on at least 20 evenings or mornings per year, and your almanac will tell you when and where to look for it. The spacecraft Mariner 10, which flew past the planet in 1974, sent back pictures showing a mountainous, cratered surface very much like that of the Moon, but Mercury has practically no atmosphere, and life there cannot exist.

Venus behaves in the same way as Mercury, but the situation is much better, partly because Venus is larger than Mercury and partly because it is much further from the Sun: 108 million km (67 million miles) on average, as against 58 million km (36 million miles) for Mercury and 150 million km (93 million miles) for Earth. Therefore, Venus' revolution period or "year" is shorter than ours, and amounts to slightly less than 225 Earth-days, though it spins very slowly on its axis and the "day" on Venus is much longer than ours. When at its most brilliant, Venus looks almost like a small lamp in the sky, and it is easy to understand why the Babylonian, Greek and Roman astronomers named it in honour of their goddess of love and beauty.

Yet lovely though Venus looks with the naked eye, it must be said to be a telescopic disappointment. As with Mercury, nothing much can be made out apart from the phase — crescent, half or gibbous. This is because Venus is covered by a dense, cloudy atmosphere, and no telescope can see through to the actual surface. The main interest for the owner of a small telescope is in following the changing phase. When Venus is in the west after sunset, the phase narrows steadily until the planet has drawn so close to the Sun that it is lost in the twilight. When Venus is a morning object, rising in the east before the Sun, the phase increases.

Make regular sketches, and you will notice something else. As the phase increases — that is to say, as Venus changes from a crescent to a half and then a gibbous form — the apparent diameter shrinks, because Venus is moving further away

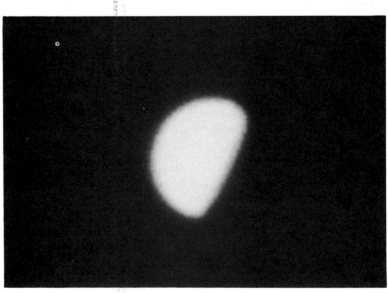

Figures 19 and 20
As Venus changes
from a crescent to a
half and then a
gibbous form the
apparent diameter
shrinks.

from us (see *Figs 19* and *20*). In fact, Venus is a most awkward object to study. Larger telescopes show occasional shady markings in the cloudy upper atmosphere of the planet, but nothing else.

The best views are obtained around sunset or sunrise, when Venus is seen against a bright sky. When the planet is low down, it is so brilliant that your telescope will show little but a twinkling mass. Certainly it is a strange place: from the spacecraft which have been there we know that there are mountains, deep valleys and active volcanoes, while thunder and lightening are almost continuous. In size and mass Venus is almost a twin of the Earth, but it is a very different sort of world.

Before the first spacecraft flew past it, we had little idea of what it was like below the clouds. Now, we have found out that it is anything but a friendly place. The surface temperature is not far short of 550°C (1000°F). The atmosphere is made up of the heavy gas carbon dioxide, which we could not breathe, and the clouds contain large amounts of the very unpleasant and dangerous substance sulphuric acid. There is no chance of finding life there, and neither does it seem likely that anyone from Earth will visit it.

Mars

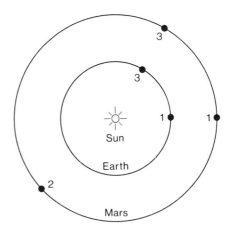

Figure 21
Oppositions of Mars.

Mars is further out from the Sun in the Solar System than the Earth is. Its average distance from the Sun is 230 million km,

(141 500 000 miles) and it can never approach the Earth to within less than 55 million km (34 million miles), which is 150 times as far as the Moon. This is a pity, because Mars is a small planet, and is only well seen for a few months in every alternate year. Its diameter is 6760km (4200 miles) so that in size it is midway between the Earth and the Moon.

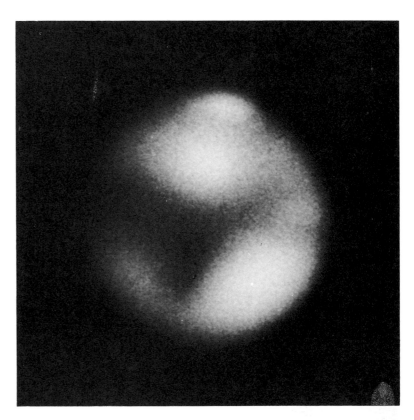

Figure 22
Mars at opposition, favourably placed for viewing.

The Earth, as we know, takes 365·25 days to go once round the Sun. Mars, moving more slowly in a larger orbit, takes 687 days. When the Earth, the Sun and Mars are more or less lined up (position 1 in *Fig 21*), the Sun and Mars are opposite in the sky. Mars is then said to be at "opposition", and is favourably placed for viewing. A year later, the Earth has been right round the Sun and has returned to position 1, but Mars has had time only to reach position 2, so that it is a long way off. The Earth has to catch Mars up, so to speak, before there is another opposition (position 3). On average this takes 780 days, so that there are long periods when the Earth and Mars are widely separated. Thus there was an opposition in 1982, and in 1984, but not in 1983 or 1985.

Oppositions of Mars

1986	July 10
1988	September 28
1990	November 27
1993	January 7

Figure 23

When at its furthest, Mars is no brighter than the Pole Star, though on the rare occasions when it is at its very closest to the Earth it may outshine all the other planets except Venus.

When looking at Mars, you will have to use the highest power that your telescope will bear: that is to say, your most powerful eyepiece. Do not be disappointed if you see little or nothing apart from a small red disk. If you manage to glimpse any dark markings, or one of the polar caps, you will be doing well. There are two moons or satellites (PHOBOS and DEIMOS), but both are less than 50km (30 miles) in diameter, and are quite beyond your range.

The time to look for detail on Mars with a small telescope is for a few weeks to either side of an opposition date. The general colour is red, which led to Mars being named in honour of the god of war (after all, red is the colour of blood), but there are darker patches, once thought to be seas but now known to be nothing more than areas which are different in colour from the surrounding red regions. The patches are permanent and have been given names. A small telescope

Figure 24
Planetary drawings of Mars showing Syrtis Major and Acidalia Planitia.

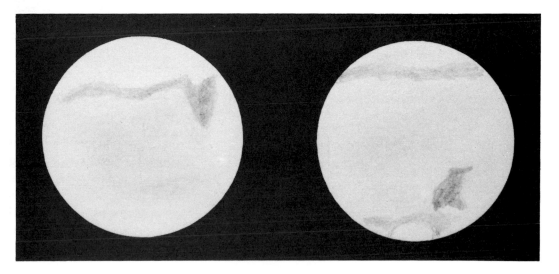

should show the two main dark markings: the rather V-shaped SYRTIS MAJOR and the wedge-shaped ACIDALIA PLANITIA in the northern (or lower) hemisphere, but much depends upon the way in which Mars is tilted, and it is not often that a small telescope will show both these markings at once, as they lie in opposite hemispheres.

The poles of Mars, like those of the Earth, are covered with ice, and when the ice-caps are at their largest they can be made out with a small telescope. They are at their best in Martian winter, and almost vanish in Martian summer. The atmosphere is thin; it can support clouds, mainly of dust, and there are times when the whole planet is hidden behind a sort of dusty veil.

Most of what we know about Mars has been discovered by the unmanned spacecraft, of which two — the Vikings — have landed there and sent back pictures direct from the surface. Mars has mountains, craters and valleys. The temperature is low, and every night is far colder than anywhere on Earth. The Martian day (which is called a "sol" by astronomers) is just over half an hour longer than ours.

It used to be thought that life might exist on Mars, but the Vikings were unable to find any, and most astronomers now believe that there is no Martian life at all. Yet the planet is much less unfriendly than Mercury or Venus, and no doubt we will go there in the, probably distant, future.

The Asteroid Belt

Beyond Mars we reach the zone of Asteroids, small, irregularly-shaped rocky bodies. Probably they are made up of material which was "left over" when the main planets were formed, about five thousand million years ago. All are very small. Only one, CERES, is as much as 1000km (600 miles) wide, and most of them look like faint stars.

The brightest of the asteroids, VESTA, is just visible with the naked eye. With your star charts it is possible to track down several others with a small telescope. The way to identify them is to check on their movements from night to night.

Jupiter

The giant of the Sun's family, Jupiter, is well beyond the asteroid belt. It is over 142 000km (88 000 miles) in diameter and more massive than all the other planets put together. Though it is a long way from the Sun — 780 million km (483 million miles) on average — its great size means that it is always very bright. Unlike Venus, it can be seen against a really dark background when it is high in the sky, and since it comes to opposition every thirteen months it is always well placed for several months in every year.

Jupiter is quite different in nature from the Earth or the other inner planets. There may be a rocky core, but it is thought that most of the planet is liquid — not water, of course, but liquid hydrogen. Above the liquid come layers of cloud, and the surface we see with a telescope is made up of gas. There are dark belts crossing Jupiter's disk, with brighter zones in between, all of which are parallel with the equator of the planet. The belts are regions where gas is sinking, while the bright zones are regions where gases are rising from below.

Because Jupiter does not have a solid surface, the markings are always changing, though there are always two belts, one to either side of the equator, together with other belts closer to the poles. When Jupiter is active, your small telescope may show four or more belts, but at least two will almost certainly be visible.

One interesting marking is the Great Red Spot, a huge oval which is more than 32 000 km (20 000 miles) long. It lies in the southern part of the planet, so that with an ordinary astronomical telescope it will be seen above the centre of the disk — provided, of course, that it is on the hemisphere which faces us. When at its most conspicuous it really is red, probably because it is coloured by red phosphorus. It is simply a vast whirling storm — a feature of Jupiter's "weather". It is not always visible. Sometimes it disappears for weeks, months or even a few years, but it always comes back, though it is smaller now than it used to be a hundred years ago, and sooner or later it will probably disappear for good.

As soon as you see Jupiter through your telescope, you will

Figures 25 and 26
As soon as you see Jupiter through your telescope, you will notice that the globe is flattened.

notice that the globe is flattened. This is because Jupiter is spinning round quickly. Its "day" is less than 10 hours long, and this rapid rotation makes the equator bulge out. If you can see any spots, or any definite markings on the belts, you will find that they drift slowly across the planet from one side to the other. The movement is slow, and it takes five hours for a feature to cross the disk completely, but if conditions are good, and you use your most powerful eyepiece, you will notice the drift after only a few minutes.

Much of what we know about Jupiter is due to four unmanned spacecraft, two Pioneers and two Voyagers, which have passed close to the planet and sent back pictures from close range. There can be no hope of sending an astronaut to Jupiter. Quite apart from the fact that there is no solid surface upon which to land, the planet is surrounded by zones of deadly radiation. Moreover, a journey there takes years; the Voyagers, launched in 1977, did not by-pass Jupiter until 1979. Eventually it may be possible to reach the larger outer satellites (see below), which are outside the worst of the radiation, but nothing of the sort is possible yet.

Satellites of Jupiter

The Voyager spacecraft also sent back pictures of Jupiter's four large satellites: IO, EUROPA, GANYMEDE and CALLISTO, which proved to be unlike anything which had been expected. All four are easy to see with any small telescope. (I even know a few very keen-sighted people who can see one or two of them with the naked eye.) They look like stars, though if you use your highest magnification you will be able to see that they are tiny disks instead of sharp points. Europa is slightly smaller than our Moon, Io slightly larger, and Ganymede and Callisto much larger; indeed, Ganymede is about the same size as the planet Mercury.

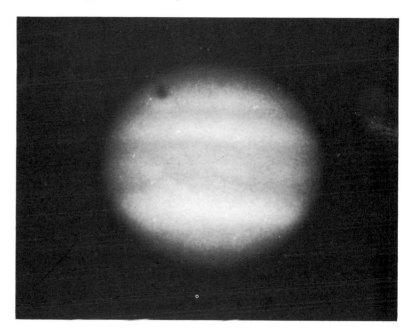

Figure 27
Ganymede is always the brightest.

The four move round Jupiter at different distances in different periods, ranging from one day and 18 hours for Io up to 1·65 days for Callisto. Because their paths lie in almost the same plane at Jupiter's equator, they are usually seen lined up. It is not hard to tell which is which. Ganymede is always the brightest, and Callisto the faintest because it is not so good at reflecting the Sun's light. Io and Europa do seem alike, but Io is generally rather the brighter of the two.

If often happens that when you look at Jupiter you will see only two or three of the satellites and, occasionally, only one. This will show that the missing satellites are either hidden or "occulted" behind Jupiter, or are being eclipsed by Jupiter's shadow, or are passing in front of Jupiter in "transit". During a transit it may be hard to see the satellite itself, but you can often see its shadow as a small black dot. It is almost as though the four satellites are playing a game of cosmic hide-and-seek.

The Voyagers showed us that the four are not like each other. Callisto and Ganymede have icy, cratered surfaces; Europa is as smooth as a billiard-ball, while Io is red, with active volcanoes hurling material high above the ground. Unfortunately these details canot be seen from Earth, even with large telescopes. The spacecraft found several smaller satellites. Altogether 12 are now known in addition to the four large ones, but are much too faint to be seen with most telescopes. Neither can we see Jupiter's ring, which is thin and dark, and was not known to exist before the flights of the Pioneers and Voyagers.

Saturn

Next in order of distance from the Sun comes Saturn, which moves at a mean distance of 1425 million km (886 million miles) and has a "year" 29·5 times as long as ours. Saturn is the only bright planet which can easily be mistaken for a star. (Venus and Jupiter are too bright to be mis-identified: Mars is very red, and Mercury is not likely to be seen at all unless you are deliberately looking for it.) It is bright, but not nearly so brilliant as Jupiter, because it is smaller as well as further away; its diameter as measured through its equator is 120 000km (75 000 miles) and, like Jupiter, it is flattened at the poles. It "weighs" as much as 95 Earths. The make-up is much the same as Jupiter's, with a solid core, layers of liquid hydrogen and then a gaseous surface, but the details on the disk are not so striking. Your telescope will probably show one dark belt, possibly two, but little else. This does not matter, because you will be able to see the wonderful ring system (see below) which is unlike anything else we know.

Rings and satellites of Saturn

The rings are not solid: no solid ring could survive, because it would be quickly broken up by Saturn's powerful pull of gravity. The rings are made up of small pieces of ice, all whirling round the planet like tiny moons. There are several main

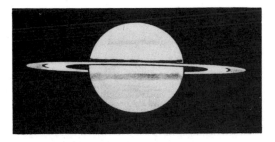

Figures 28 and 29
Planetary drawings of
the rings of Saturn.

rings; a small telescope will show two, separated by a gap called the CASSINI DIVISION (in honour of the Italian astronomer who first saw it over three hundred years ago).

Though the rings are very wide — about 435 000km (270 000 miles) from one side to the other — they are also very thin, and when they are placed edge-on to the Earth, as last happened in 1980, they almost disappear. At such times they cannot be seen at all with small telescopes, and even large instruments show them as nothing more than a thin line of light. Luckily, the ring-system will be well placed between now and the late 1980s, so that this is a good time to start looking at Saturn.

Figures 30 and 31
This is a good time to
start looking at
Saturn.

Like Jupiter, Saturn has a whole family of satellites. Twenty are now known, but only one of them is really large. This is TITAN, bigger than our Moon, and bright enough to be seen with a small telescope. The Voyagers showed that it is a remarkable world, with a thick, cloudy atmosphere and quite possibly liquid oceans on its surface, though it is so cold that no life can be expected there. It takes nearly sixteen days to complete one journey round Saturn, and its movements can be followed from night to night. You may also be able to glimpse two other satellites, IAPETUS and RHEA, but they are not easy with a telescope of aperture less than 75mm (three inches), so that you will probably have some difficulty in finding them.

Uranus, Neptune, Pluto

Finally we come to the three planets discovered in more modern times; URANUS (in 1781), NEPTUNE (1846) and PLUTO (1930). Uranus and Neptune are giants, smaller than Jupiter or Saturn but still much larger than the Earth, while Pluto is smaller than the Moon, and probably made up chiefly of ice. With a star map you will be able to find both Uranus and Neptune, but they will look like stars, though Uranus may be distinguished because of its greenish colour. All their satellites are comparatively faint. Pluto, incidentally, has an orbit which is much less circular than those of the other planets, and at present it is actually closer-in than Neptune. It takes 248 years to go once round the Sun.

There may well be another planet further out than Neptune and Pluto. Most astronomers believe that it exists, because it would explain why some other planets move along the courses that they do. But even if it is there, it is bound to be very faint and hard to find. At present, therefore, Neptune and Pluto mark the boundary of the main part of the Solar System.

Programme 4:
Observing Comets and Meteors

The Solar System contains many other objects as well as the Sun, the planets and their satellites. In particular there are COMETS, which are not solid and rocky; they are made up of small pieces of material (mainly ice) together with "dust" and very thin gas. A bright comet has a head and one or more tails; the GREAT COMET of 1843, for instance, had a tail that stretched more than half-way across the sky.

Comets move round the Sun, but their paths are not almost circular, as with the planets. Instead they move in long, narrow eclipses. We know of dozens of comets of short period, so that we always know when and where to expect them, but because of their faintness it cannot be said that they are of much interest to the owner of a small telescope. We also know of many other comets with periods of from five up to 100 years, but with one exception they are dim and few of them ever develop tails of any length. A comet may develop a tail as it comes in toward the Sun. The ice in its head evaporates and streams out to make the tail, which always points more or less away from the Sun. This is due to the radiation streaming out from the Sun (the "Solar Wind"), so that when the comet is travelling outward it moves tail-first.

The really brilliant comets seen now and then have periods of hundreds or thousands of years, so that they cannot be predicted, and take us by surprise. Several were seen in the last century, but there have been far fewer in the past 80 years.

Encke's Comet

Encke's Comet, named after the German astronomer who first worked out how it moves, has a period of only 3·3 years, and is seen regularly. Because a comet depends for its sparkle upon light from the Sun, it is visible only when it is moving in the inner part of the Solar System. The path of Encke's Comet takes it from inside the orbit of Mercury but nearly as far as Jupiter. A small telescope will show it when it is at its best, but it will look like a hazy patch, and there will be no tail.

Halley's Comet

There is one long-term comet. Halley's, which is a bright naked-eye object and takes only 76 years to go round the Sun. It has a history going back at least to 1066 (it was illustrated in the Bayeaux Tapestry), and was identified in 1682 by Edmond Halley. It was last on view in 1910, and is due again in 1986. In fact it was picked up, as a very faint blur of light, as early as October 1982. It will become visible in a small telescope around the autumn of 1985, and by late November should be easy to see with the naked eye. It reaches its closest point to the Sun in February 1986, after which it begins to move outward again; after about April 1986 it will have faded below naked-eye visibility, but with your telescope you should be able to follow it well into the summer. Unfortunately Halley's Comet will not be at its best at this return, because the Earth and the Comet are in the wrong places at the wrong times, but at least it will be interesting, and it is expected to produce a fairly long tail. To observe it you will need a wide field of view, which means using a low-powered eyepiece. There may be interesting changes in the tail, and these can be tracked, though if the tail is really long it may be that the best views of it will be obtained with binoculars.

Meteors (shooting stars)

Meteors are tiny particles, usually smaller than grains of sand, moving round the Sun. If a meteor dashes into the Earth's upper air, at a height of roughly 195km (120 miles), it rubs against the air particles and is headed by friction, so that it burns away, causing the streak of light which we call a shooting star. Every time the Earth passes through a swarm of meteors we see a shower of "shooting stars". The best shower is that of early August, known as the PERSEID SHOWER because the meteors appear to come from the direction of the constellation Perseus (see page 68).

Telescopes are of no use for observing meteors: the best way to watch for them is by naked-eye watching. If you stare upward on a dark, clear night any time between 29 July and 15 August you will be very unlucky not to see at least one meteor. Of course there are many other showers, and there are also meteors which do not belong to showers at all. Very occasionally a really brilliant meteor is seen. I once saw one which took several seconds to cross the sky, and was brighter than the full moon. It was probably about the size of a walnut!

Nor is there any fear of being injured by a meteor, because these tiny objects burn away at over 65km (40 miles) above the ground. It is true that we meet with occasional larger bodies which land as solid lumps, and may even make craters. There is a crater almost a mile wide in Arizona, formed over 20 000 years ago, and others in Siberia, Australia and Arabia, but these "meteorites", made up chiefly of iron and stone, are not associated with ordinary meteors, and may well have come from the Asteroid Belt. Most museums have meteorite collections, but there is no reliable record of anyone having been killed by a tumbling meteorite.

Artificial satellites

There are also artificial satellites, or "man-made moons", of which many hundreds have been launched since the start of the Space Age on 4 October 1957, when the Russians sent up their first satellite, the football-sized Sputnik 1. Satellites shine because they catch the sunlight. They move much more slowly than meteors, and may crawl so gradually that they can be mistaken for ordinary stars, though a very few minutes observation is always enough to show that a satellite is travelling slowly against the starry background.

I have often had letters saying: "I saw an object crossing the sky last night; can it have been a comet?" The answer is "No", because a comet is well outside the Earth's atmosphere and you have to watch it for hours before you can notice any shift against the stars. Anything which moves noticeably must be either a meteor or else an artificial satellite (unless, of course, it is a weather balloon or a high-flying aircraft).

How to Find the Stars

Now that we have looked at the members of the Solar System, and decided what your telescope will show, it is time to turn to the stars. Here the problems are quite different. To see the Moon or planets really well, you need calm steady air, so that the image does not shift around. For the stars, we need a sky which is really transparent. This often happens after a heavy rainstorm. The stars then seem brilliant, but the air may well be so disturbed that the details on the planets cannot be seen at all.

The stars are suns, some of them much larger, hotter and more luminous than ours; they appear so much smaller and fainter only because they are so much further away. With the naked eye they cannot be seen in the daytime, because of the brightness of the sky, and the light of the full Moon will also drown all but the more brilliant stars.

A star which is low down in the sky will twinkle. This has nothing to do with the star itself. Twinkling is caused by the Earth's unsteady atmosphere, which affects the rays of starlight as they pass through. A star near the horizon shines through a thick layer of atmosphere while a star near the overhead point or "zenith" sends its light to us through a much less extensive layer, so that it twinkles less. Planets twinkle less than stars, because they appear as tiny disks rather than sharp points, but it is quite true to say that a planet will twinkle noticeably when it is low down.

The Sun is a single star. Other stars may be double and there are also multiple stars. Some stars are variable in brightness, and we also find stars which suddenly flare up to become brilliant for a few days, weeks or months before fading back to their original state.

Magnitude (brightness) and colour

The scale of apparent brightness is known as "magnitude". The lower the magnitude, the brighter the star. Thus bright stars are of magnitude 1. Stars of magnitude 2 are fainter, magnitude 3 fainter still, and so on. The faintest stars normally visible with the naked eye on a clear night are of magnitude 6. A 50mm (two-inch) refractor will show stars down to magnitude 9, perhaps even 10 under excellent conditions, while the faintest stars which can be recorded with the world's largest telescopes are of about magnitude 25. At the other end of the scale there are a few stars which are brighter than magnitude 1, so that they have zero or even negative values. Sirius, the brightest star in the sky, has a magnitude of minus 1·4, while on the same scale the magnitude of Venus can reach minus 4·4, and the Sun is about minus 27.

The stars are not all alike. In particular, they are of different colours. Our Sun is yellow, while Rigel in the constellation of Orion is white, and Betelgeux, also in Orion, is orange-red. These differences are due to differences in surface temperatures; 6000°C in the case of the Sun, 12 000°C for Rigel, but only about 3000°C for Betelgeux.

There are a few stars whose colours are easy to notice with the naked eye (Betelgeux is a good example), but the colours are much better seen with a telescope or binoculars. Here, a reflector is better than a refractor: even a good refractor will produce a certain amount of false colour around a bright star, while a reflector will not — it will show the star's colour as it really is.

Nebulæ and the life of stars

Stars are born inside the clouds of gas and dust which we call NEBULÆ. As they shrink, because of the effects of gravitation, they become hotter and denser. When they are sufficiently hot inside, they begin to shine. The core temperature at this stage is about ten million degrees Centigrade. As we have seen, a star such as the Sun is radiating because it is changing one element (hydrogen) into another (helium), losing mass as it does so. Stars which are more massive than the Sun use up their "fuel" more quickly, so that they do not last for so long.

After a Sun-like star has used up all its available hydrogen, it has to alter its structure. Its core shrinks, and its outer parts swell out and cool: the star becomes a Red Giant, as Betelgeux is now. Eventually the star may throw off its outer layers altogether, and all that is left is a very small, feeble star which is amazingly heavy. Stars of this kind are called White Dwarfs. If I could fill an egg-cup with material from a White Dwarf, it would weigh several tons.

A star which is much more massive than the Sun will explode violently as soon as it has used up all its energy reserves, and will end up as a patch of expanding gas around a tiny object even smaller and heavier than a White Dwarf. Explosions of this kind are called supernovæ. Unfortunately you are not likely to find one in our Galaxy yet awhile; the last to be seen in the Milky Way system blazed out as long ago as the year 1604. If we have a star which is more massive still, it will not explode, but will shrink down until not even light can escape from it — and we are left with what is called a Black Hole, cut off from the rest of the universe.

Stars of the four seasons

Your telescope will show you clusters of stars, nebulæ, and even a few of the outer galaxies. But before you can appreciate them properly, you will have to find your way around the constellations. This is not nearly so difficult as might be thought. The best plan is to start with a few groups which are very easy to recognize, and use these as pointers to the rest.

There are some constellations which never set over our part of the northern hemisphere because they are too near the North Pole of the sky. These include the Great Bear, the Little Bear, and the W-shaped constellation of Cassiopeia. Internationally, astronomers use the Latin names of the constellations, so that the Great Bear becomes Ursa Major, the Little Bear is Ursa Minor, and so on. It is just as well to get used to these names at once, because there is nothing difficult about them, but I will also give you the English equivalents.

So let us work our way through the year in the next section, Programme 5, seeing what stars are visible in the evening sky. The planets, remember, move around, but they always keep to a definite belt in the sky known as the ZODIAC, which is divided into twelve constellations. If you see a bright object in a Zodiacal constellation, and cannot identify it from your map, you may be fairly certain that it is a planet, but there is little risk of being misled. Venus and Jupiter are too brilliant to be mistaken; Mars is always very red, and you will not see Mercury at all unless you make a deliberate search for it. Only Saturn can easily be confused with a star.

Programme 5: Observing the Stars

Northernmost stars

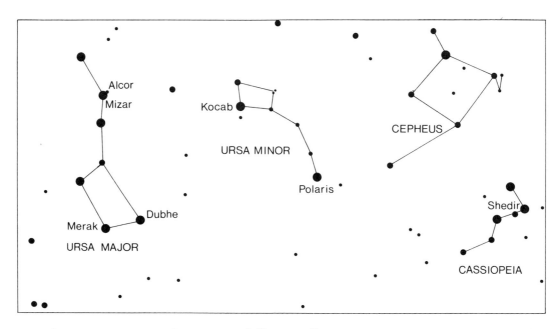

Star Chart One:
Northernmost stars

The easiest of all constellations to recognize is URSA MAJOR, the Great Bear — sometimes nicknamed the Plough or, in America, the Big Dipper. Its famous pattern is made up of seven stars. Six of them are of about the second magnitude, while the seventh is somewhat fainter. Even at its lowest (as during evenings in autumn) the Great Bear is always well above the horizon, so that you can always find it whenever the sky is sufficiently dark and clear.

Now use your telescope. Look first at the second star in the Great Bear's tail. Its name is MIZAR, and even with the naked eye you should be able to see a much fainter star, ALCOR, close beside it. Binoculars show the two well, and with your telescope you will see that Mizar itself is double; there are two Mizars, one rather brighter than the other, so close together that with the naked eye they appear as one star. (See Variable stars on page 71.)

Next, turn your telescope to the stars at the other end of the Great Bear, MERAK and DUBHE, known as the POINTERS because they show the way to the Pole Star. With the naked eye you will see little difference between them except that Dubhe is rather the brighter. As soon as you use the telescope, you will see that while Merak is white, Dubhe is definitely orange, so that its surface is the cooler of the two.

Now follow up the line from Merak through Dubhe. It will lead you straight to POLARIS, the Pole Star, in the constellation of URSA MINOR, the Little Bear, which also is white. It has a faint companion, just visible with a two-inch telescope. Polaris is a very powerful star, shining 6000 times as brightly as the Sun, but it is also a long way away. Its distance is almost 700 light-years, so that we are now seeing it not as it really is, but as it used to be seven hundred years ago, when Edward I was King of England.

Next, trace the outline of the Little Bear, which curves down over the Great Bear's tail. There is one star in it, KOCAB, which is about as bright as Polaris or Mizar. Use your telescope, and you will see that, like Dubhe, it is orange rather than white. The other stars of the Little Bear are faint, and when the Moon is near full you will not be able to see them with the naked eye, though they are obvious enough against a dark sky.

The third important constellation of the far north is CASSIOP-EIA, whose five main stars form a wide W or M (whichever you prefer). Four of them are white, the fifth, SHEDIR, is orange. Like the Bears, Cassiopeia never sets over Britain.

On a dark night you will see that Cassiopeia is crossing by the lovely band of the MILKY WAY. Use your telescope — putting in your lowest-power, widest-field eyepiece — and you will see that the Milky Way is made up of stars. There are so many stars that to count them would be impossible, and you might well think that the stars must be in danger of bumping into each other.

Yet this is not true. As we noted on page 8, the Milky Way's appearance is due to our looking along the main thickness of the flattened Galaxy, and seeing many stars in almost the same direction. However, your telescope will show you the most magnificent star-fields anywhere along the Milky Way band, and Cassiopeia is a good place to begin.

Winter stars

On winter evenings the Great Bear lies in the north-east. Use the Pointers to find the Pole Star; next, a line from Mizar through Polaris will show you the position of Cassiopeia. But in the southern part of the sky there is an even brighter constellation: ORION, named after the hunter of ancient legend.

Of the leading stars in Orion, two are particularly bright: BETELGEUX in the upper left, RIGEL in the lower right. I have already said something about Betelgeux, which is a huge Red Giant, even though it still looks like a point of light with your telescope. Then look at Rigel, which is even more powerful, and is equal to 60 000 Suns put together. The difference between the two is striking.

Next, find the three second-magnitude stars of the HUNTER'S BELT. Below them lies the SWORD, marked by a magnificent gaseous nebula, known as M42 because it was the forty-second object in a list of star-clusters and nebulæ drawn up 200 years ago by the French astronomer Charles Messier. You can see the nebula with the naked eye on a clear night, and your telescope shows it well: there is bright gas, together with darker patches. The Orion Nebula is a stellar birthplace. Look for four stars close to its edge; these make up the TRAPEZIUM, and are so hot that they make the dust and gas in the rest of the nebula shine.

There are many other nebulæ of the same kind, but M42 is probably the most beautiful of them all when seen through a small telescope. It is about 1500 light-years away, and although the dust and gas is very thinly-spread it hides objects deep inside the nebula. We know that powerful stars exist there, but we can never see them even with our most powerful telescopes, though there are other ways of locating them by using radio and X-ray techniques.

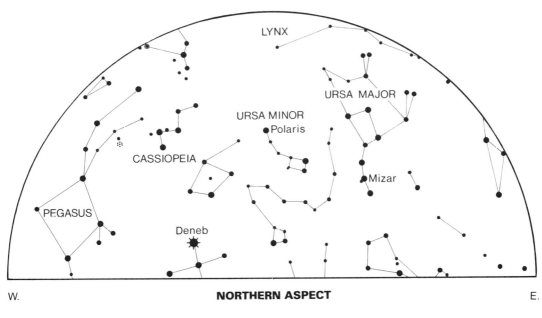

NORTHERN ASPECT

W.   E.

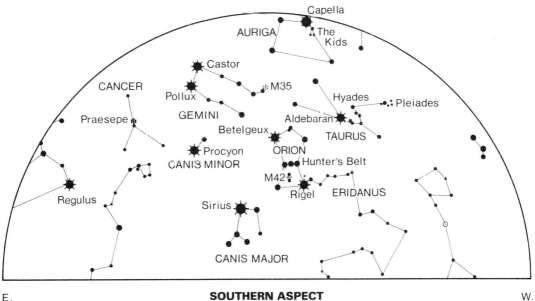

SOUTHERN ASPECT

E.   W.

Star Chart Two:
Winter stars

Follow the line of the Belt downward, and you will come to SIRIUS, which twinkles violently because it is so brilliant and is always rather low down as seen from Britain. It is the leader of the constellation of CANIS MAJOR, the Great Dog. Actually, Sirius is not nearly so luminous as either Betelgeux or Rigel, but it is still 26 times as powerful as the Sun. It is one of the nearest of the bright stars, and lies at a distance of only eight and a

Figure 34
A V-formation of faint stars making up the cluster known as Hyades.

half light-years, which works out at roughly 85 million million km (50 million million miles). It has a White Dwarf companion, but a small telescope will not show it, because it is so overpowered by the brilliance of Sirius itself.

Upward, the Belt stars show the way to ALDEBARAN in the constellation of TAURUS, The Bull, which, like Betelgeux, is orange-red. Close beside it is a V-formation of faint stars, making up the cluster known as the HYADES. The cluster is real, but Aldebaran does not really belong to it; it lies about half-way between Hyades and ourselves.

To look at "open clusters" of this sort, use your lowest-power eyepiece, because it will give you the widest possible field of view. With a higher power, you will see only a few stars of the cluster at once, and the full beauty will be lost.

Beyond Aldebaran there is an even more beautiful open cluster, the PLEIADES or Seven Sisters, also in Taurus. To the naked

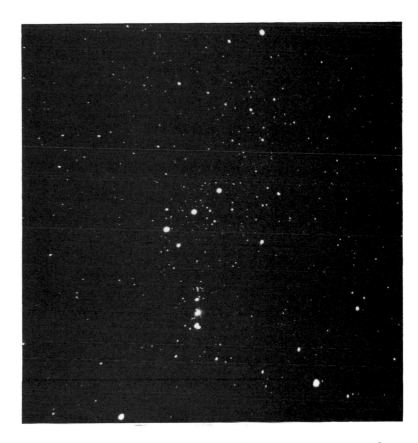

Figure 35
The best views of the Pleiades are got by using the wide field provided by binoculars.

eye they appear as a hazy patch. Most people can see at least seven separate stars without binoculars, and your telescope will show dozens, most of them hot and white. Again, use your lowest magnification. In fact, I believe that the best views of the Pleiades are got by using the wide field provided by binoculars — far wider than that of any telescope.

Taurus is in the Zodiac, so that planets may pass through it. So is the constellation of GEMINI, the Twins, which can be found from Orion: a line drawn from Rigel through Betelgeux will show the way to it. The two brightest stars are CASTOR and POLLUX. Pollux is of the first magnitude, Castor of the second — and here again the colours are different, because Castor is white and Pollux orange. Castor is a double star (see Variable stars on page 71).

The rest of the Twins is made up of lines of fainter stars stretching towards Orion. Beyond two of them is the open cluster M35. You should be able to find it easily. It is not so rich or so large as Pleiades, but it is certainly worth looking at.

Between the Twins and Sirius there is another bright star, PROCYON in the constellation of CANIS MINOR, the Little Dog. Further east is a much fainter constellation, CANCER, the Crab, which is also in the Zodiac. The Crab contains a lovely open cluster, PRÆSEPE or the Beehive, which is just visible with the naked eye and will be well shown by your telescope.

Almost overhead during winter evenings you will see a very brilliant star, CAPELLA in the constellation of AURIGA, the Charioteer. You cannot mistake it, because it is so bright. It is yellow, like the Sun, but is much more luminous. Close beside it you will be able to make out a triangle of faint stars, known as the KIDS.

In the west during winter evenings may be seen another interesting constellation, PEGASUS, the Flying Horse, whose four leading stars make up a large square, but Pegasus is better on view during autumn evenings, when it is higher up in the sky (see page 68).

Spring stars

By mid-April Orion has almost disappeared into the evening twilight and it will be out of view all through the summer, because it will be too near the Sun in the sky. Castor and Pollux in Gemini are still to be seen, the Great Bear is practically overhead, and the W of Cassiopeia is low in the north.

Follow round the curve of the Great Bear's tail, and you will come first to ARCTURUS, a very brilliant star in the constellation of BOÖTES, the Herdsman. It is a lovely sight in your telescope, because of its light orange colour. Not far from it is the little constellation of CORONA BOREALIS, the Northern Crown, which is easy to find because of its shape — even though only one of its stars, ALPHEKKA, is as bright as the second magnitude. In the "bowl" of the Crown your binoculars, or wide-field telescope, will usually show two stars. One of these is of magnitude 6·6, just too dim to be seen with the

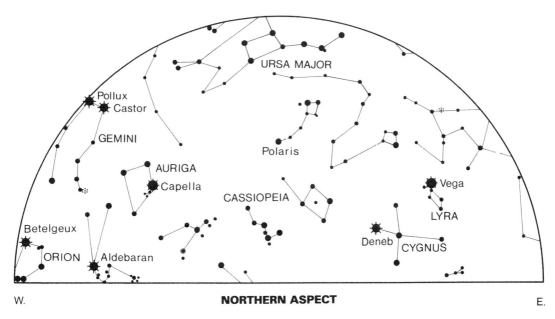

NORTHERN ASPECT

W.　　　　　　　　　　　　　　　　　　　　　　　　　　　　　E.

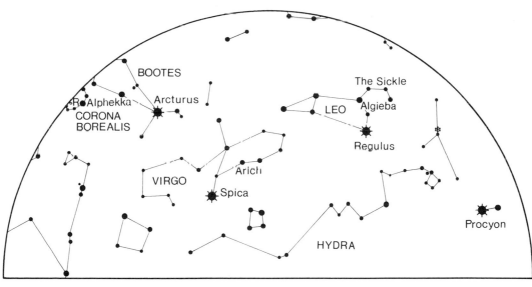

SOUTHERN ASPECT

E.　　　　　　　　　　　　　　　　　　　　　　　　　　　　　W.

Star Chart Three:
Spring stars

naked eye. The other, R CORONÆ, is a remarkable variable star, and is described on page 72.

Continue the curve from the Bear's tail through Arcturus, and you will come to a white first-magnitude star, SPICA in the constellation of VIRGO, the Virgin. Virgo is a very large constellation and is included in the Zodiac. Spica is its only really bright star, but you will be able to make out a Y-formation of fainter stars, one of which, ARICH, is of special interest as a binary or twin star system which looks as if it were closing in as one (see page 72).

If you use the Pointers in the Great Bear "the wrong way" — that is to say, away from the Pole Star — they will lead you to the constellation of LEO, the Lion, with its bright leader REGULUS. Regulus lies at the bottom of a pattern of stars known as the SICKLE, arranged rather like a question-mark as seen in a mirror. One of these stars, ALGIEBA, is also a double, but not in the same way as Arich (see page 73).

Brilliant Capella is sinking in the west. On the opposite side of the Pole Star, and about the same distance from it, is the blue star VEGA in the little constellation of LYRA, the Harp. During summer evenings Vega is almost overhead, while Capella is very close to the northern horizon, but neither actually sets as seen from Britain.

Summer stars

Summer evenings are obviously less suitable for star-gazing than those of other seasons, because the nights are so much shorter. Also, we have lost Orion and its brilliant companions. The Great Bear lies in the north-west. Leo and Virgo are dropping toward the western horizon. Arcturus is high, and the overhead position is occupied by Vega.

Aiming a small refractor at Vega in this position is not easy unless the telescope is mounted upon a platform or a very high tripod, because the eyepiece will be so low down, but Vega is worth seeing, because of its lovely, steely-blue colour. And although Lyra is a small constellation, it is an interesting one. Close to Vega is a faint star known as EPSILON LYRÆ. People with keen sight can see that Epsilon is double, and the two members of the pair are well seen with even a low magnification on your telescope.

The two brightest stars in Lyra, apart from Vega, are BETA LYRÆ and GAMMA LYRÆ. They are easy to find: Gamma is the brighter of the two, while Beta is somewhat variable. Directly

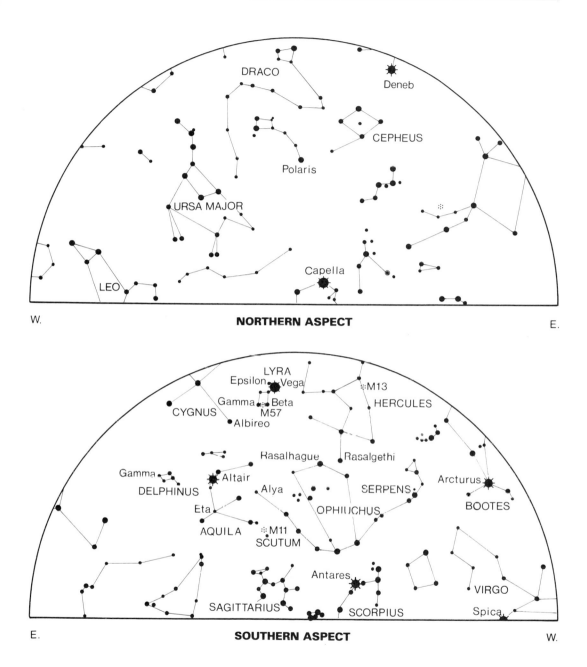

NORTHERN ASPECT

W. E.

SOUTHERN ASPECT

E. W.

Star Chart Four:
Summer stars

between them lies the RING NEBULA, M57. This is not in the least like the Orion Nebula. It is simply a very old star which has shed its outer layers, so that it has surrounded itself with a ring of expanding gas. It is not bright, but your telescope will show it unmistakably, and you may even be able to see the ring, looking like a tiny, luminous cycle tyre, but larger instruments are needed to show the faint, hot central star.

The Ring is the best example of a "planetary nebula" (a bad name, because it is not truly a nebula and is certainly not a planet). Others can be found, but most of them are fainter than the Ring, and are less conveniently placed for the inexperienced observer.

Vega is one of three brilliant stars well placed during summer evenings. The others are ALTAIR in the constellation of AQUILA, the Eagle, and DENEB in the constellation of CYGNUS, the Swan. Altair, high in the east, is easy to identify because it has a fainter star to either side of it. Also in the constellation there is one star, ETA AQUILÆ, which is of special interest because it is variable (see page 73).

At the lower end of the Aquila pattern there is another lovely star-cluster, M11, known as the Wild Duck cluster. It is fan-shaped, and excellently seen with a moderate power, while with a higher power the individual stars in it are very clear. M11 is not actually in Aquila, but in the small constellation of SCUTUM, the Shield, but Aquila is the best guide to it.

To the east of Altair you will find the compact little group of stars making up the constellation of DELPHINUS, the Dolphin. In 1967 a faint star in the Dolphin suddenly brightened up until it had become visible with the naked eye. It was discovered by a well-known amateur astronomer in England, George Alcock. This was a NOVA. Nova means "new", but novæ are not really new stars. A typical nova system is made up of two stars, of which one is a very old White Dwarf. The dwarf pulls gas away from its larger companion until the situation becomes very unstable. There is a sudden explosion, and the system increases rapidly in brightness, though it soon dies down to its old state. The nova in the Dolphin is still visible, but its magnitude is now below 11, so that your 50mm (two-inch) telescope will not show it.

The last bright nova flared up in the Swan in 1976. It became brighter than the Pole Star, but remained visible with the naked eye for only a few nights, and has now become very faint indeed. This constellation is itself often called the NORTHERN CROSS, and certainly its main stars make up a well-defined X. DENEB, the leader, is a real starry searchlight, at least 60 000 times as powerful as the Sun. One star of the X, ALBIREO, is fainter than the rest and further away from the centre of the constellation, but to make up for this it is probably the most beautiful double star in the sky (see page 73).

Much of the southern part of the summer sky is occupied by two large, faint constellations, HERCULES and OPHIUCHUS. Ophiuchus, the Serpent-bearer, has one star of the second magnitude, RASALHAGUE. Close to it is RASALGETHI in Hercules, which is variable between magnitudes 3 and 4, and is very red. Look also for the globular cluster M13. The chart shows where to find it. It is on the limit of naked-eye visibility, and your telescope will show that it is quite unlike an open cluster such as the Pleiades. A globular cluster is a "ball" of stars, so crowded near the centre of the cluster that they merge into a blur of light. If our Sun lay near the middle of a globular cluster there would be many stars in the sky bright enough to cast shadows, and there would be no proper darkness at all.

Finally, look low in the south. There you will find the bright red star ANTARES in the constellation of SCORPIUS, the Scorpion, which is a Zodiacal constellation. Like Altair, Antares has a fainter companion to either side, but you cannot possibly confuse the two, because Antares is lower down and stands out at once because of its colour. It is the reddest of the really brilliant stars. East of the Scorpion is the constellation of SAGITTARIUS, the Archer, also in the Zodiac. It has no first-magnitude star, but the Milky Way is very rich here. In fact, the centre of the Galaxy lies behind the Sagittarius star-clouds, so equip your telescope with its lowest power and sweep along the whole area. You will see that the star-fields are as rich as any to be found in the sky, and it is a pity that Sagittarius is always low down from Britain.

Autumn stars

During autumn evenings, the Great Bear is at its lowest, which means that the W of Cassiopeia is nearly overhead. In the east, the Pleiades have come into view, followed by Aldebaran. Arcturus has disappeared below the western horizon, but Vega, Deneb and Altair are still fairly high. Capella is rising in the east as Vega drops toward the west. Very low down in the south you will see the first-magnitude star FOMALHAUT

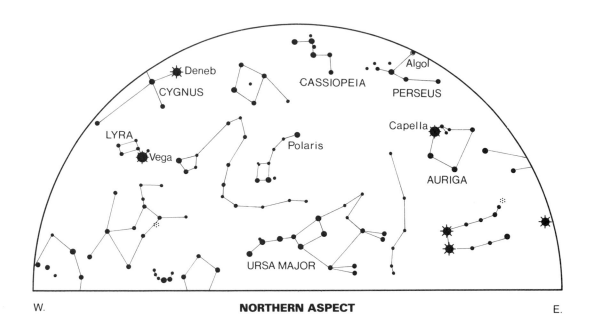

W.   **NORTHERN ASPECT**   E.

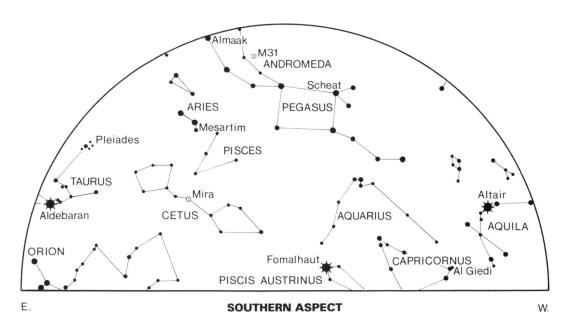

E.   **SOUTHERN ASPECT**   W.

Star Chart Five:
Autumn stars

in the constellation of PISCIS AUSTRINUS, the Southern Fish, but much of the southern part of the sky is taken up by large, dim Zodiacal constellations: PISCES the Fishes, AQUARIUS the Water-bearer, and CAPRICORNUS the Sea-goat. Turn your telescope to AL GIEDI in Capricornus: it is a wide, easy double star, and keen-eyed observers can separate it without using binoculars.

The chief autumn constellation is PEGASUS, with its famous square shape. Three of its leading stars are white, while the fourth, SCHEAT, is orange, as you will notice at once if you look at it through your telescope. Like many giant stars of its type, it is somewhat variable.

Not far from Pegasus, and also in the Zodiac, is the constellation of ARIES, the Ram. Of its three main stars, the faintest, MES-ARTIM, is a wide, easy double (see page 73).

Leading away from Pegasus is the line of brightish stars marking the constellation of ANDROMEDA, where we find M31, the Great Spiral, which is an independent galaxy, so far away that its light takes over two million years to reach us. It is, in fact, the most remote object which can be clearly seen with the naked eye.

Figure 39
Through a telescope
M31 is disappointing.

Photographs taken with large telescopes are needed to show its shape properly. But it is the brightest of the outer galaxies ever visible from Britain, so find it by all means, and marvel at it — particularly since you are looking two million years backward in time — but do not expect too much. When a newcomer visits my observatory, one of the objects I am always asked to show is M31. Naturally I agree (provided that M31 is

above the horizon!) but it must be admitted that through a telescope M31 is disappointing, as it looks like nothing more than a faint smudge.

M31 is a huge system. It is larger than our Galaxy, and it contains about one hundred and fifty thousand million stars, as well as clusters, nebulæ and all the features which we know in our own Galaxy. Like our Galaxy it is a spiral, like a Catherine-wheel, though unfortunately it lies at a narrow angle to us, and the full beauty of the spiral is lost.

There are more objects of the autumn sky which deserve mention. One is the double cluster in the sword-handle of

Figure 40
M31, the Great Spiral, so far away that its light takes over two million years to reach us.

Figure 41
The double cluster in
the sword-handle of
Perseus

PERSEUS, a constellation lying between Andromeda and Capella (not to be confused with the Sword or Orion). Here we have two rich clusters so close together that they lie in the same low-power field of your telescope.

Finally, in your exploration of the autumn sky, you should try to locate two interesting objects which will be mentioned again in more detail in the next section. One is ALGOL, also in Perseus, and the other is MIRA CETI, in the constellation of CETUS, the Whale, which can only be seen for few weeks in every year: catch it then and memorize its position against the nearby stars.

Variable and binary stars

As you scan the night sky more and more thoroughly with your telescope you will discover that some of those millions of pin-points of light are very strange objects indeed. It would be a good idea if, after becoming generally familiar with the layout of the planets and stars, you made a special survey of the variable stars and the double or "binary" star systems on their own. There is much to be surprised at in their behaviour! Let us follow the same order as in the sections you have just read.

In the Northernmost stars we found MIZAR, next to Alcor in the Great Bear. Mizar is a splendid example of a binary. The two stars move together round their common centre of gravity or balancing point; the best example I can give is the way in which the two bells of a dumb-bell move if you twist them by the arm which joins them together — though in the case of Mizar, one full revolution takes many centuries instead of only a second or two.

In the Winter stars we noted that one of the two brightest stars in the constellation of the twins, CASTOR, is a double star. It is difficult to separate with a small telescope, but with your highest power you should be able to see that it does not look quite like an ordinary star.

In the Spring stars, I said that R CORONÆ, in the Northern Crown, is a remarkable variable: generally it is brighter than its neighbour, but sometimes it literally puffs out clouds of soot, which hang in the star's atmosphere and dim its light. At such times R Coronæ cannot be seen at all without a large telescope — so if you look, and find that it is missing, you will know that it is going through one of its sooty periods!

The binary ARICH in the Virgin (also in the Spring stars) looks with the naked eye like an ordinary star of the third magnitude, but your telescope will show that it is made up of two, exactly equal in every way — real stellar twins. They form a binary system and take 180 years to complete one journey round their "balancing point". When I first looked at Arich, about fifty years ago, it was one of the widest binary pairs in the sky. Today we see it at a less favourable angle. Though your 50mm (two-inch) telescope will still separate them, conditions are becoming more difficult, so that by the end of the century Arich will appear single except when observed with very powerful instruments. After the year 2116 the separation will start to increase again.

The other double star which I mentioned in the Spring stars is ALGIEBA in the constellation of the Lion. One member of the pair is much brighter than the other. The brighter star is orange, its companion slightly bluish. You may have some difficulty in seeing both stars, but it should be possible if you use one of your higher-power eyepieces.

The faint EPSILON LYRÆ, in the constellation of the Harp, which I mentioned in the Summer stars, can be seen as a pair by low magnification. Now use your most powerful eyepiece, and you may be able to see that each member is again double, so that we have a double-double or quadruple star. All four are at the same distance from us (about 120 light-years). I admit that I have great difficulty in seeing all four stars with any telescope smaller than a 75mm (three-inch) refractor, but those people with keener eyes may have better luck. BETA LYRÆ, also near Vega, is another easy double, though this time the two members are unequal in brightness.

In the Eagle there is ETA AQUILÆ, which brightens and fades regularly, being at maximum every seven days. The magnitude ranges between $3\frac{1}{2}$ and $4\frac{1}{2}$, so that it is always visible with the naked eye. Another fine double star, ALYA in the constellation of SERPENS, the Serpent, can also be found near Aquila. Here again we have perfect stellar twins, absolutely alike in every way.

In the constellation of the Dolphin (Summer stars) too we have a good example of a double star: GAMMA DELPHINI, a yellowish star with a fainter companion which has a tinge of blue.

ALBIREO in the Swan (Summer stars) should not be missed: there is nothing else quite like it. If you have any difficulty in finding it, remember that it lies slightly away from a line joining Vega to Altair. Any small telescope will show that Albireo is a golden-yellow primary together with a companion which is of a glorious blue.

In the Autumn stars, the Zodiacal constellation of the Ram has the double star MESARTIM with its members exactly equal, although to the naked eye it looks like an ordinary star well below the third magnitude.

Andromeda (Autumn stars) too has an easy double star, ALMAAK, with an orange primary and a bluish companion. It is not nearly so easy to split as Mesartim in the Ram, but it is worth looking at. You may have to use your highest magnification to separate it clearly.

Also in Perseus is ALGOL, which is normally about as bright as the Pole Star, but which gives a long, slow "wink" every two and a half days, fading down by over a magnitude in a period of four hours and remaining faint for 20 minutes before starting to recover. Algol is not a true variable. It is a binary, with one member much brighter than the other. Every two and a half days the fainter star passes in front of the brighter one, which explains why Algol winks.

I must say a little about MIRA CETI, the Wonderful Star in the Whale. It is variable, with a period of 331 days (that is to say, one maximum is followed by another 331 days later, though admittedly the period is not absolutely constant). At its best Mira may become as bright as the Pole Star, but at minimum it drops to the tenth magnitude, at the limit of your small telescope. Like almost all long-period variables, it is a huge Red Giant.

Mira is a naked-eye object for only a few weeks in every year. Memorize its position against the nearby stars; then, as it fades, you will be able to follow it as it drops towards minimum. Mira, unlike Algol, is a true variable, swelling and shrinking, and changing its output of energy as it does so. There are many variables of this kind — and we may be thankful that our own Sun is such a steady, well-behaved star!

Steps towards an observatory

Permanent mounting

The simple altazimuth telescope, with which we have been dealing in this book, is portable, and can be carried around without much difficulty. With a larger telescope things are much less convenient, and it may be wise to make a permanent mounting outdoors. This can be either in the form of a tripod or a pillar, firmly fastened down (by concrete, for instance). It is then possible to carry the telescope out, and set it up, each time it is to be used, but there are dangers here, because it is only a question of time before something gets dropped, with disastrous results. Merely covering up the telescope with a tarpaulin or something of the kind, and leaving it permanently outdoors, is not really to be recommended, on account of condensation and other troubles (see Care and maintenance on page 19).

Run-off shed

Professional observatories are usually graceful domes with revolving roofs, but a much simpler solution is the run-off shed. The shed covering my own 320mm (12½-inch) reflector is made in two halves, which run back on rails in opposite directions and leave the telescope in the open.

This is a better design than a single shed with a door at one end, partly because the single, heavier shed is less easy to roll back, and partly because the door is a nuisance. If it is hinged, it is liable to flap, and if it is removable, putting it back in place in the dark can be a problem — in a high wind the door may act as a powerful sail. At any rate, my run-off shed has given me no trouble at all since it was made in 1947. If no rails are available, angle-iron will do, and small wheels are easy to find. The shed may be of hardboard covered with roofing felt, though wood is obviously better.

Equatorial mounting

Figures 42 and 43
The shed covering my own 12½-inch reflector runs back on rails to leave the telescope in the open.

A more advanced type of telescope mounting is upon an axis which is parallel with the axis of the Earth. In other words, the axis points to the north pole of the sky, marked within a degree by Polaris. This is a help, because when the telescope is being swung from east to west (or west to east) the "up or down" movement looks after itself. Adding a clock drive, to compensate for the rotation of the Earth, makes the telescope automatic, and it can then be used for photography, when you have acquired a more powerful telescope — at least a 75mm (three-inch) refractor or 150mm (six-inch) reflector.

Careers in astronomy

Amateur astronomers need no formal qualifications, and, as in the case of George Alcock's discovery of the nova in the Dolphin, they can make themselves really useful. Professional astronomy is essentially mathematical, and there is no chance of obtaining a post in astronomy (or any other science) without taking a degree. In general, I advise would-be astronomers to take a basic first degree in physics, because this is sufficient for most posts in astronomy, and a degree in pure astronomy can be added if required. Either way, the first needs are the usual GCE O-Levels, together with A-Levels in at least mathematics, physics and another science subject. Once these have been passed, you can start a degree course. Of course, it is possible to take a first degree in pure astronomy, but unless you are absolutely certain that you want to be a professional astronomer it is sensible to take a physics degree first, because it gives you a much wider scope, and after you graduate you may have to wait for some time before you find a post in astronomy which would suit you.

Astronomical societies

I strongly recommend joining an astronomical society. In Britain there are two national societies mainly for amateurs; the British Astronomical Association, Burlington House, Piccadilly, London, W1 and, for younger enthusiasts, the Junior Astronomical Society. Most large towns and cities also have local societies, listed in the annual *Yearbook of Astronomy* (Sidgwick & Jackson), which should be found in any Public Reference Library. If you decide to join, you will not only make many friends, but you will also be able to exchange observations — and an observation is of no use unless other people know about it, so that they can use it if they wish.

Some "Don'ts"

These are from my own experience; others may disagree, but I think that what follows is sensible.

1. **DON'T** spend too much time on astronomy when school examinations are close ahead, particularly if it means staying up late. You will have plenty of time later.

2. **DON'T** go outdoors, and spend hours in a cold wind, without making sure that you are properly clothed. If you are shivering, and your hands are numb, you will in any case find it difficult to make good observations.

3. **DON'T** neglect your telescope. Make sure that it is carefully treated, and if you are using a reflector check the lining-up of the mirrors before starting work. If anything seems to be badly wrong, take the advice of an expert.

4. **DON'T** expect to see much by poking a telescope through an open window. The heated air from inside will swirl out and ruin the seeing. Observing from the roof of a heated house is not much better.

5. **DON'T** expect too much. You will not see anything like the lovely coloured pictures of planets, star-clusters and nebulæ given in so many books. But you will see much that is of tremendous interest, and there is never any shortage of objects to observe.

6. **DON'T** be unsystematic. Log your observations carefully, and enter them in your notebook as soon as you have finished. If you leave the copying-in until later, mistakes are bound to creep in.

And, lastly, most important of all:

7. **DON'T EVER** look straight at the Sun, even with a dark filter fitted to the eyepiece of your telescope.

Index